THE SHADOW NATION

Strategic Culture of Pakistan's Deep State

THE SHADOW NATION

Strategic Culture of Pakistan's Deep State

Harsh V Singh

Foreword by

Tilak Devasher

PENTAGON PRESS LLP

First published in 2025 by
PENTAGON PRESS LLP
206, Peacock Lane, Shahpur Jat
New Delhi-110049, India
Contact: 011-26490600

Typeset in Century Schoolbook, 11 Point
Printed at Aegean Offset Printers, Greater Noida

ISBN 978-81-987484-4-7

www.pentagonpress.in

To the brave hearts I had the honour to lead,
and to the commanders whose courage, wisdom,
and patience shaped my own.

This book is a tribute to those who walked the
harshest paths without hesitation,
without expectation and bound by the credo:

"Your country's safety, honour, and welfare come
first, always and every time.

The honour, welfare, and comfort of the men you
command come next.

Your ease, comfort, and safety come last,
always and every time."

Contents

Foreword

Strategic culture is a conceptual framework that helps understand the behavioural tendencies and policy preferences of any institution, especially military. This framework is particularly relevant in examining the Pakistan Military, whose institutional identity has become entwined with the political, religious and ideological characteristics of the Pakistani state over the years. This incisive book by Harsh provides a thorough analysis of the development of that strategic culture, its internal challenges, and its external implications; especially regarding India-Pakistan relations.

The strength of his work lies in its interdisciplinary approach, drawing from history, political science, and sociology. As a practitioner of military warfare, he has been able to chart the metamorphosis of the Pakistan Army from a post-colonial military bureaucracy into a complex entity, wielding disproportionate influence over national policy. The analysis interrogates foundational myths, martial race theory, ideological exceptionalism and civil-military fusion. He traces their institutionalisation from Partition to the present day, particularly through the militarisation of Islam under General Zia-ul-Haq and the subsequent entrenchment of the military in Pakistan's economic and political spheres.

What distinguishes this book is its careful attention to the contentious relationship between societal trajectories; ethnicity, sectarianism, political disenchantment and institutional adaptation within the Pakistan Military. It underscores how these factors are not merely peripheral forces but central to understanding the mutation of strategic culture, especially under the current doctrinal posture associated with General (now Field Marshal) Asim Munir. The empirical grounding provided by original survey data and doctrinal analysis further strengthens the work's relevance to both academic and policy-making communities.

In an era where South Asia remains a locus of strategic volatility, the implications of a revisionist military culture in Pakistan extend well beyond its borders. For India, and indeed for global stakeholders, this work offers critical insights into the behavioural logic of a nuclear-armed military establishment under considerable internal duress. Its concluding section, which outlines actionable policy options across diplomatic, economic, and military domains, is particularly salient for those seeking a stable modus vivendi in the region.

This book is a valuable addition to the growing body of literature on strategic culture of Pakistan's Deep State and subcontinental geopolitics. It invites scholars, practitioners, and policymakers to engage with the layered realities that define one of the world's most enduring strategic rivalries.

In conclusion, let me admit that I may be biased since we both share our academic journey from the portals of Mayo College. Nevertheless, I do extend my sincere appreciation to Harsh for his outstanding work. His deep and nuanced understanding of military affairs and ability to present complex issues with such clarity and insight make this book an invaluable contribution to the field. It's rare to come across a work that is both intellectually rigorous and practically relevant, and ***The Shadow Nation*** succeeds on both fronts.

Tilak Devasher

Preface

Let me begin with a story—one that shaped the course of how I think. It was the summer of 1986. I had returned home from boarding school, full of opinions and adolescent confidence. During a family discussion about *Bharat Ek Khoj*—the acclaimed TV series based on Pandit Jawaharlal Nehru's *The Discovery of India*. I, with impetuousness declared the book 'outdated'. My grandfather, Dr. Shiv Mangal Singh 'Suman', a celebrated poet and academic, said nothing at first. Instead, he quietly walked into his study, brought me a copy of the book, and with a calm resolve said, "Read this before you return to school. We'll talk then. Never speak about something you haven't understood."

That moment left a mark. Since then, I've carried one lesson with every uniform I've worn, every appointment I've teneted, and every paper I've read: never form an opinion on half-baked knowledge.

This pursuit of deeper understanding led me to this book—and to Pakistan.

Over the last three decades in uniform, one idea has remained constant: know thy enemy—a timeless dictum from *Sun Tzu*, often quoted, rarely internalised. We've studied Pakistan superficially in India—through headlines, ceasefires, skirmishes and summits. However, few have explored the DNA of its national behaviour—its strategic culture. Fewer still from a practitioner's lens.

This book is an attempt to do just that.

The Pakistan Army is not just a stakeholder in the country's power matrix—it is the matrix. Since its inception in 1947, it has shaped the country's worldview, defined its red lines, rewritten its political script, and, over time, become the guardian of the national identity, Nazariya-e-Pakistan rooted more in insecurity than in nationhood. It is the architect of the Deep State—the enduring, shadowy force that dictates how Pakistan behaves, reacts, and survives.

The Shadow Nation explores how that strategic culture has evolved—mutated, even—under the weight of external pressures, domestic instability, ideological dogma, and shifting regional dynamics. It doesn't claim to be the final word. Instead, it asks difficult questions, connects the dots, and invites readers, especially those in uniform, policy, research, or diplomacy, to re-evaluate what they think they already know.

Unlike many existing works, this is not a detached academic critique, nor is it merely a war memoir. It is a convergence of military experience and intellectual inquiry—of battle maps and bibliographies. It draws from strategic theory, regional history, open-source data, and personal conversations to paint a complex but accessible picture of how the Pakistan Army perceives itself and how that perception guides its conduct.

If you are starting your journey of understanding India's most persistent adversary, or looking to revisit your assumptions with fresh eyes, this book is for you.

In writing it, I owe a debt of gratitude to every mentor, soldier-scholar, and analyst who challenged my thinking, opened archival doors, and debated with unflinching honesty. The errors, omissions, or blind spots are entirely mine.

What began as a question has grown into a reflection. This reflection now stands as a call to look deeper, listen closer, and understand better—not just the nation that lies across the border but the shadows that define it.

Harsh V Singh

Acknowledgements

Writing a book is often perceived as a solitary pursuit—but, in truth, it is a journey shaped by many voices, countless conversations, and a web of silent supporters who walk beside the author, even when unseen.

This book originates from the academic space and intellectual freedom I was granted at the National Defence College (NDC). The thesis I wrote there became the scaffolding for this work. I remain profoundly grateful to the NDC faculty for their unwavering guidance, critical feedback, and quiet encouragement, especially during moments when this project felt daunting. Your mentorship provided not just direction but conviction.

To the thought leaders and academicians whose scholarship challenged and inspired me, your work served as both compass and catalyst. Engaging with your ideas allowed me to sharpen my own.

I also express my deep gratitude to the mentors in the Armed Forces who nurtured intellectual inquiry, trusted in the merit of strategic debate, and provided the time, space, and resources that allowed this book to take its present form. To my exceptional cohort of **NDC-64**, your honest reflections, rigorous debates, and enduring camaraderie were the lifeblood of this inquiry. Many may not realise how your questions and critiques helped shape this book.

Finally, to my family. Thank you for your silent strength, your patience through my long absences, and your unshakable belief in this effort. Your presence was my anchor in the noise of research, writing, and revision.

This book is not the final word on the subject, but it is a sincere attempt to understand a nation and an institution that continues to cast its long shadow across our strategic horizon. If this work provokes thought, invites scrutiny, or initiates further inquiry, then it will have served its purpose.

Harsh V Singh

One

Introduction

> *"The professional soldier in a Muslim Army, pursuing the goals of a Muslim state, cannot become 'professional' if in all his activities he does not take on the colour of Allah"*
>
> —General Zia-ul-Haq[1]

General

Christine Fair in her book *Fighting to the End*, has branded the "Pakistan Army as a revisionist army not satisfied with the status quo".[2] The evolution of the Pakistan military from an imperial army of the British Raj to a jihadi army has been attributed to General Zia abetted by the JeI. However, on deeper study, this revisionist mental framework or Islamic orientation was germinated by British officers post Partition and it gained further credence with the creation of Bangladesh; a "*strategic shock*"[3] suffered by the Pakistan military. The strategic culture of the Pakistan military has a direct impact on Pakistan's security calculus, and foreign policy and may be considered an appropriate prism through which Pakistan's status in South Asia needs to be reviewed.

It is pertinent to define 'Strategic Culture' to establish a framework and commonality of lexicon. Ken Booth, a British international relations theorist, has defined strategic culture as

"A nation's traditions, values, attitudes, patterns of behaviour, habits, customs, achievements and particular ways of adapting to the environment and solving problems concerning the threat or use of force."[4] On 9 May 2023, branded as 'Black Day'[5] by the Pakistan military, the bastion of Pakistan military became vulnerable to internal stressors for the first time in 75 years. The election on 8 February 2024 has dented the supremacy paradigm cultivated by GHQ, Rawalpindi, wherein the writ of the military failed in many quarters.[6]

The strategic culture of the Pakistan military is based on a historical frame of reference, that is, Pakistan's Lebensraum.[7] This is inextricably linked to the unfinished business of Partition in which Pakistan believes it was denied its rightful share due to a conspiracy orchestrated by the Nehru-Mountbatten nexus. In the normative domain, the Pakistan military has evolved into a self-serving and self-preserving cabal that is suffering from an onslaught of societal vectors mutating its strategic culture and codifying its present behaviour largely on postulates of the Munir doctrine[8] articulated by the current COAS. The Pakistan Army's raison d'être is the perpetuation of the idea that they are the custodians of '*Nazariya-e-Pakistan.*'[9] This thesis aims to analyse the strategic culture of the Pakistan military, the effect of societal stressors on it, and impact on India-Pakistan interaction in the conflict continuum.

Fault Lines

Ethnicity. Conventional wisdom in and about the Pakistan military has been that the dominant Punjabis had co-opted the Pashtuns as a junior partner to rule the roost; a proverbial Batman-and-Robin equation of the 'super hero' and his loyal sidekick. This détente has frayed due to the political fissures with Pakistan's polity voting in the February elections along ethnic lines. The targeted killing of Punjabis[10] in KPK and the eviction of Afghans from Pakistan (Fig. 1)[11] have further exacerbated the ethnic fissures. The interplay of the ethnic fault

Fig. 1: Eviction of Afghans from Pakistan

lines and its impact on the Pakistan military's strategic culture remains to be explored. A disproportionately large number of the top level positions in the Pakistan Army are still held by Punjabis. Eight to nine Chiefs of Army since Pakistan's independence have been Punjabi, including the present incumbent, General Munir. There is a deep-set resentment against the 'Punjabi army' among other ethnic groups. The Punjabis in the army have also been accused within Pakistan itself of suppressing sub-regional ethnic politics, especially after East-Pakistan became Bangladesh. The same is true for the current Baloch movement. In 1948 and 1958, massive force was used by the army against the Baloch rebellion. In 2007, when General Pervez Musharraf was in charge, Nawab Akbar Bugti (Baloch leader) was killed in a military operation which was heavily criticized by the general public. In addition to the above, there is another strong reason why the army, from being protectors of their people, slipped into the role of being the sole rulers of the country. The areas that constituted West-Pakistan after Partition lacked highly skilled bureaucrats, lawyers, advisors and technicians necessary for the development of the country. These positions were hence filled by educated migrants from British India. These migrants left India as they feared democracy would dissipate their privileges. The people of Punjab were not willing to hand over power into the hands of uneducated locals who outnumbered them. In essence, democracy did not suit the financial health of the feudal lords and was detrimental for the ruling elite of Pakistan. It also brought with it the threat that an 'inferior race' of Bengalis who were more in number, may end up ruling Pakistan. Therefore, the elite ruling class of Pakistan was unwilling to hand over power to the Bengalis or any other ethnic minority. In 1958, the Pakistani army officially came into power, even though it had shared power with the elite in Pakistan for nearly a decade before that. During the period 1958 to 1971, the Pakistani army began strengthening its roots and consolidating its grip on power in Pakistan while the political scenario was unstable and chaotic with repeated changes of the government. "It is important to note that Pakistan's armed forces especially the army operates like a fraternity. In this environment, severe punishments to individuals or extraordinary treatment of a similar nature are viewed as undermining the morale of the institution. Sidelining undesirable individuals or rewarding others discreetly is, thus, a preferred choice," Ayesha Siddiqa-Agha, security analyst of Pakistan writes.

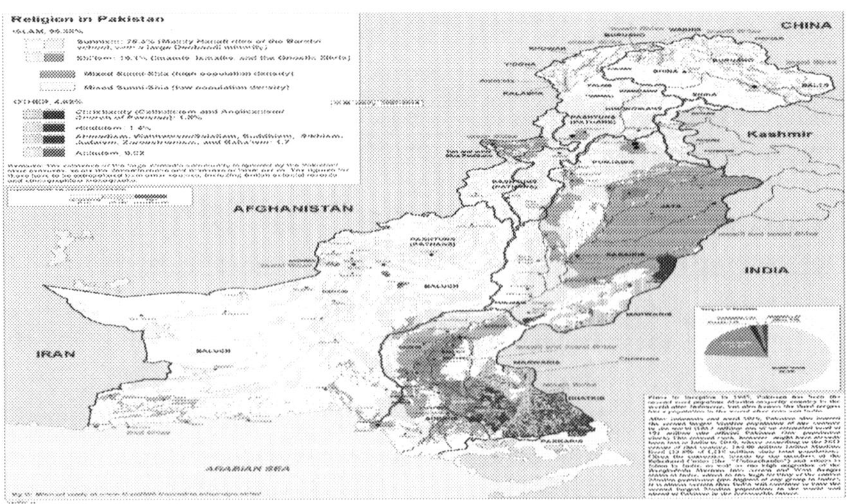

Fig. 2: Religious Land Scape

Sectarianism. Pakistan is in the eye of the storm with fault lines between Shia and Sunni religious competitors in this 'Land of the Pure.' Nazariya-e-Pakistan is the epitome of modern global Muslim aspiration and forms a crucial component of the narrative but the chasm remains. The impact of a larger sectarian schism may not impact the Pakistan Army as the Shia presence in the armed forces is extremely limited; however, what remains to be studied is the impact of the intra-sect difference between the Barelvi and Deobandi sects of Sunni Islam. The rise of TLP as an agitational terrorism force[12] as a counter to Deobandi dominance merits review. The Deobandi sect is more aligned to the fundamentalist Salafi strain of Islam being exported by Saudi Arabia as the Pashtuns are more aligned to the Deobandi sect and the Punjabis to the Barelvi sect that is more tolerant, coalescing the ethnic and sectarian fault lines. Religious radicalism led to an attempted coup by Major General Zaheer ul Islam Abbasi in 1995. Abbasi, who, along with 35 other conspirators, was arrested on 26 September 1995, failed to kill the Pakistan Army's senior leadership when it had assembled for the corps commanders conference chaired by the army chief. The ostensible aim of the coup was to overthrow what Abbasi saw as an un-Islamic regime.[13]

Neo-Feudalism in Pakistan

Pakistan has a long-standing tradition of feudalism, characterized by the dominance of powerful landlords. These feudal lords have wielded significant control over the general population, exerting their influence over various aspects of regional economic, political, and social progress. Their families hold immense wealth, influence, and political power, granting them extensive authority over the lives of ordinary individuals and can easily be branded as the 'elite' of Pakistan. The neo-feudal landlord of Pakistan is the army, which by many statistical references, holds 12 per cent of all arable land in Pakistan.[14] This land holding allows the Pakistan Army to fashion the local narrative of the people. COAS

General Asim Munir has shown an unusual personal interest in the venture of 'corporate farming'[15] and the army has even created new agro subsidiaries such as FonGrow[16] headed by retired army generals who have created a niche as neo-feudals in Pakistan under the aegis of its Fauji Foundation. In July 2023, it also inaugurated a 'State-of-the-Art Corporate Agriculture Park' spread over 2,250 acres in Pirowal in Punjab.[17] Similar plans for ushering in agricultural prosperity have been made for the barren Cholistan desert where the use of modern technology for sustainable farming and establishment of agri-malls for agricultural commerce is on the anvil. Messrs Green Corporate Initiative Pvt. Ltd., another subsidiary of the Pakistan Army's MILBUS has acquired approximately 52,000 acres of land spread across six districts for corporate farming. The 52,713 acres of 'barren' land include 28,000 acres in Khairpur, 10,000 acres in Tharparkar, 9,305 acres in Dadu, 1,000 acres in Thatta, 3,408 acres in Sujawal and 1,000 acres in Badin.[18] This vast tract of land will be handed over to the GHQ-owned firm for the next 20 years to execute its 'Green Pakistan Initiative'.

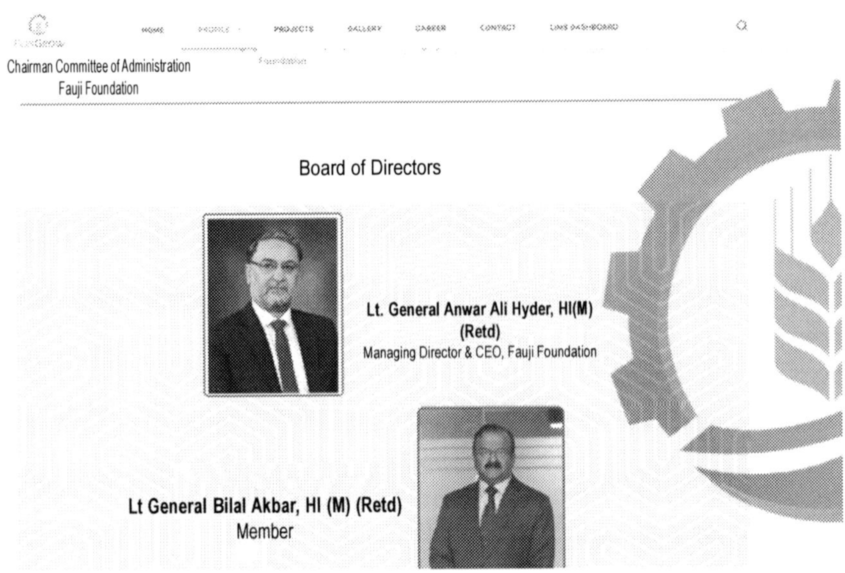

Fig. 3: Hierarchy of FONGROW

The neo-feudal nature of the Pakistan military has also impacted its strategic culture as it is steeped in the business and banking sectors, thus making the economic sustenance of Pakistan a key enabler for its survival, both as an organization and also as individuals. Ayesha Sidiqia in her book, *Military Inc* (2017), has focused on the business enterprise of the military in Pakistan but fails to account for the impact this neo-feudalism is bound to have on the strategic culture of the Pakistan military. The aim of the Pakistan military is to protect their business conglomerate and that has led to their penetration in every facet of economic activity in Pakistan including the acquisition of land.[19] SIFC[20] with the COAS and PM of Pakistan as members of the apex committee[21] along with the military presence at each level of execution alludes to the fact that economics would be a key governing factor towards the strategic behaviour of the Pakistan military and needs to be studied.

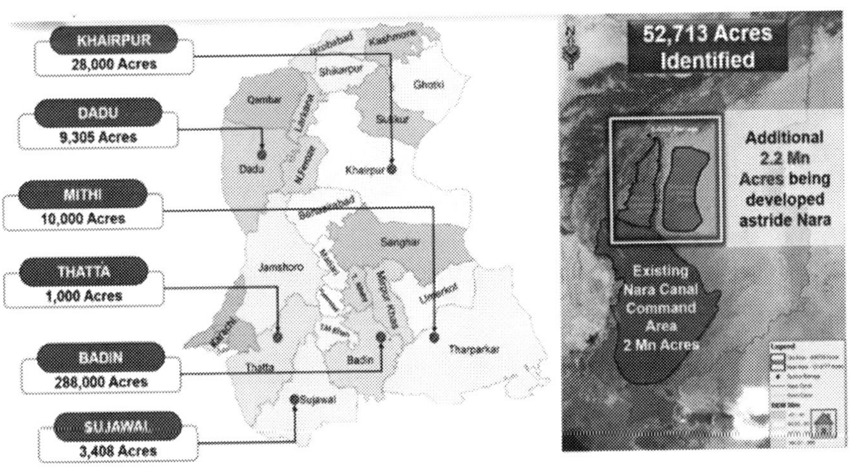

Fig. 4: Land Acquisition by Pakistan in Sindh[22]

While land acquisition in Pakistan is being pursued relentlessly as an institution, the provision of land as an incentive for service in the armed forces allows personnel of the Pakistan Army to take possession of land in prime locations. In his 2008 book, *Crossed Swords: Pakistan, Its Army, and the Wars Within*,

Shuja Nawaz mentions how a self-created 'culture of entitlement' is rampant in the military, especially amongst its top brass. Last year, while ruling on a case regarding the federal government's housing project, Justice Qazi Faez Isa of Pakistan's Supreme Court invoked this book saying that even though gifting land did not have any constitutional or legal sanction, "nevertheless, senior members of the armed forces get plots and agricultural lands and continue to be given additional plots and agricultural lands as they rise up the ranks."[23] Records of all land along the borders is maintained by the Border Area Committee (BAC). Its chairman is an army officer of brigadier or colonel rank with an assistant commissioner as the civil member assisted by a revenue officer (tehsildar) and his staff. The BAC projects the requirement of land to the concerned Provincial Board of Revenue (PBR), which, in turn, passes on the details to the District Collector (DC). The DC sends the same to the establishment officer who issues the land allotment order. On retirement, the Pakistan Army offers gratis land to its veterans which automatically catapults them into the realm of the feudal elite. The residential and agricultural land allocated to Pakistan Army veterans is given below:

Service (in yrs)	Residential Land
15	First plot
25	Second plot
28	Third plot
32	Fourth plot

Residential Land Allotment[24]

Rank	Land Allocation (Acres)
Maj Gen & above	240
Brig & Col	150
Lt Col	124
Maj	100
JCO	64
NCO	32

Agricultural Land Allocation[25]

Effect of War on Terror

The Pakistan military, since 2001, has been running with the hare and hunting with the hounds as far as the war on terror is considered. Repeated efforts by the Pakistan armed forces to rein in the terrorist outfits operating on its western borders in the form of Operation Al Mizan,[26] Operation Rah-e-Nijaat, Operation Zarb-e-Azb, Operation Radd-al-Fasad[27] and Operation Azm-e-Estakam have impacted the strategic culture of the Pakistan military, both on the professional front where the focus has shifted from conventional to sub-conventional warfare and at the societal level as a stressor concerning martyrdom and concept of supreme sacrifice in the name of the nation and religion operating at divergence. Maria Rashid, in her seminal work, *Dying to Serve* (2020), writes about *Mazhab-ka-shaheed* and *Desh-ka-shaheed* but the lasting effect of this rift would need further analysis.

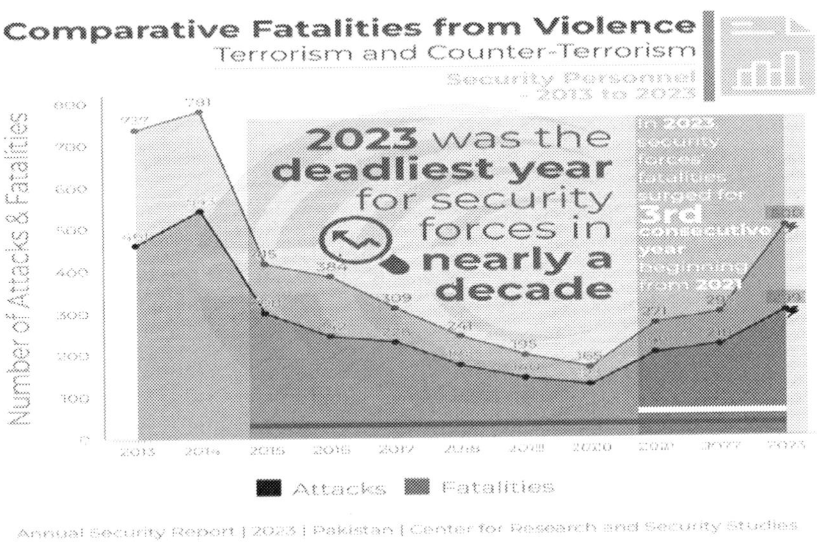

Fig. 5: Terrorist Attacks in Pakistan[28]

NOTES

1 Malik SK, The Quranic Concept of War, Himalaya Books, N Delhi, 1976, 1986, p. 02 (Foreword).

2 Fair Christine, Fighting to the End: The Pakistan Army's Way of War (Oxford, UK: Oxford University Press, 2014), p. 21.

3 Freior Nathan, Known Unknowns: Unconventional Strategic Shocks in Defence Strategy Development, Carlisle Strat Studies Institute, 2008, pp. 04-05.

4 Booth Ken, "The Concept of Strategic Culture Affirmed," in Strategic Power: USA/USSR, ed. Carl G. Jacobsen (London: The Macmillan Press, Ltd., 1990), p. 125.

5 https://tribune.com.pk/story/2416010/may-9-is-historys-dark-chapter-army accessed on 22 Feb 24.

6 Malik, Adeel, and Maya Tudor. "Pakistan's Coming Crisis." *Journal of Democracy* 35, no. 3 (2024): 69-83. https://doi.org/10.1353/jod.2024.a930428 accessed on 03 Jul 24.

7 Friedrich Ratzel, a German geographer and ethnographer coined the concept of Lebensraum, or "living space," which relates human groups to the spatial units where they develop. Ratzel pointed out the propensity of a state to expand or contract its boundaries according to rational capabilities.

8 https://thefridaytimes.com/04-Sep-2023/the-munir-doctrine-blast-bulldoze-disregard-all-obstacles-to-economic-recovery accessed on 23 Dec 23.

9 https://www.dawn.com/news/741890/nazariya-i-pakistan accessed on 22 Feb 24.

10 https://www.ndtv.com/india-news/6-barbers-kidnapped-shot-dead-by-terrorists-in-pakistans-khyber pakhtunkhwa accessed on 06 Mar 24.

11 https://www.aljazeera.com/news/2023/10/4/pakistans-plan-to-evict-thousands-of-afghans-unacceptable-says-taliban accessed on 03 May 24.

12 Sareen Sushant, *Tehrik-E-Labbaik Pakistan: The New Face of Barelvi Activism* (2023), *ORF Occasional Paper No. 332*, September 2021, Observer Research Foundation.

13 Cloughley, Brian, *A History of the Pakistan Army Wars and Insurrections*, Lancer Publishers andDistributors, Second Edition, p. 352-353.

14 https://www.spectator.co.uk/article/the-military-millionaires-who-control-pakistan-inc/ accessed on 01 May 25.

15 https://risingkashmir.com/pakistan-armys-feudal-interest-in-agriculture/ accessed on 03 May 25.

16 https://fongrow.com/About/#FonGrowTeam accessed on 04 May 25.

17 https://risingkashmir.com/pakistan-armys-feudal-interest-in-agriculture/ accessed on 03 May 25.

18 Ibid.

19 https://www.farmlandgrab.org/post/31760-pakistan-seeks-6bn-for-corporate-farming-from-saudi-arabia-other-gulf-nations-by-2028 accessed on 23 May 24. Major General (retired) Tahir Aslam, MD & CEOof FonGrow (subsidiary of Fauji Foundation) is planning to acquire 100,000 acres of land for corporate farming.

20 https://investmentpolicy.unctad.org/investment-policy-monitor/measures/

4366/pakistan-establishes-the-special-investment-facilitation-council-sifc-accessed on 05 Mar 24.

21 https://thegeopolitics.com/pakistans-military-extends-its-role-in-economic-decision-making-through-the-special-investment-facilitation-council/ accessed on 22 May 24.

22 Sushil Tanwar, Fighting to Farming: Pakistan Military's Relentless Quest for Relevance, https://www.orfonline.org/expert-speak/fighting-to-farming-pakistan-military-s-relentless-quest-for-relevance accessed on 23 May 24.

23 https://brighterkashmir.com/news/pakistan-armys-culture-of-entitlement accessed on 01 May 25.

24 https://theprint.in/opinion/security-code/pakistan-army-has-two-loves-flag-of-islam-and-land-gen-bajwas-loot-isnt-new/1231081/ accessed on 12 Dec 24.

25 https://www.dawn.com/news/1043051/farm-land-allotment-scheme-for-army-officers accessed on 14 Oct 24.

26 Terrorism and Pakistan's response (tribune.com.pk) accessed on 05 Mar 24.

27 https://www.criticalthreats.org/analysis/pakistans-counter-militant-offensive-operation-raddul-fasaad accessed on 25 Feb 24.

28 https://crss.pk/pakistans-violence-related-fatalities-mark-a-record-6-year-high-56-surge-in-violence-recorded-in-2023-crss-annual-security-report/ accessed on 23 May 24.

Two

Framework of Pakistan Military's Strategic Culture

The Radcliff Line created angst of an immense proportion for the ideologues of Pakistan for getting a '*moth-eaten*' version of Pakistan.[1] Pakistan's elite maintained that the evil Indian was bent on eradicating the new state and re-absorbing in India.[2] Pakistan, during Partition, was fraught with misconceptions and an overarching nihilism about distribution of assets;[3] only seven of the 46 training establishments were attributed to Pakistan.[4] The commission to divide assets had legislated that 170,000 tons were to be despatched in 300 trains but only three trains arrived in Pakistan.[5] After the deaths of Jinnah and Liaquat Ali Khan,[6] the Muslim League, bereft of second-tier leadership, had to abdicate power to the military. With firm support from the feudal community, the Pakistan military asserted itself in the country's politics without any political experience. The Pakistan military ran the country like a defence establishment, and this led to the creation of a strategic culture which permeated Pakistan society as well. The strategic culture of the Pakistan military is ipso facto the strategic culture of Pakistan as scripted by Stephen Cohen in his book, *Idea of Pakistan*.[7]

Inimical India

The signing of the Instrument of Accession by the ruler of J&K was also an Indian conspiracy to deny Pakistan its rightful territorial space. The subsequent war in 1947-48 and the performance of the Pakistan military to protect the Muslim homeland against Hindu India became the pillar of the Pakistan military's strategic culture manipulated by the military and the elite.[8] Even the national anthem of India was a rallying point that India would still like to re-integrate Sindh back into India,[9] 'Punjab, *Sindh*, Gujarat, Maratha, Dravid, Utkal, Banga, Vindhya, Himachal, Yamuna Ganga."[10] India as the putative adversary is a time-tested ploy to divert the populace from societal concerns such as social inequality, sectarian (Sunni-Shi'a) rupture, and the distinct absence of HDI in Pakistani society.[11]

India's animosity is reflected in the Afghan refusal to accept the Durand Line as a border with Pakistan. This got exacerbated by the hosting of an 'All India Pashtun Jirga' in 1951 at New Delhi and allowing the Afghan ambassador to defame Pakistan in a speech broadcast on All India Radio.[12] The USSR's President Khrushchev visited Kabul in 1955 and expressed his sympathy with the Afghan policy of '*Pashtunistan*' and provided 300 million USD of military aid.[13] The assassination of Liaquat Ali Khan by an Afghan[14] and USSR support to Afghanistan at India's behest calcified the precept of anti-Pakistan India. The offensive launched by Afghanistan in Bajaur Agency of FATA in September 1960 was viewed by the Pakistan military as an attempt to open two fronts by India.[15] While the Afghan offensive may have failed, the complicity of India was reinforced by the state machinery to further vitiate the atmosphere.[16] This vitriolic vision of India again crystallized during the Indus Water Treaty which was also considered as an Indian conspiracy.[17]

Pakistan's identity was tied to the idea of a 'Muslim Homeland', so much so that the head of the PML, Chaudhary Khaliquzzaman suggested a pan-Islamic unity of countries to be known as 'Islamistan'.[18] While Jinnah had viewed a secular strain in Pakistan when addressing the Pakistan constituent assembly,[19] the same was hijacked by the Ulema led by Abu-al-Ala-al-Mawdudi, the founder of the Jammat-e-Islami, who pushed for adoption of an Islamic constitution.[20] A Hindu India will never allow Pakistan to prosper and co-exist. This angst has been reiterated over the three wars which, as per Pakistan perception, were thrust upon them by India. It is with this deep-rooted hatred that the Pakistan military sees India as a putative adversary for eternity. The nation has been bred on a daily dosage of hatred for India[21] and fanned by the Pakistan military to maintain its primacy as the last bastion of resistance.

The Pakistan Army is still smarting over the loss of Bangladesh in 1971, the occupation of Saltoro Ridge in 1984,[22] the reversals in 1999 in Kargil sector, the climb-down during Operation Parakram in 2002[23] and the recent responses by Indian forces to terrorist attacks in 2016 and 2019.[24] These reversals have bred many generations of the Pakistan Army with hostility against India and keeping them unhappy with the territorial arrangements on the subcontinent. Despite Pakistan's unwillingness to accept the territorial status quo in South Asia and hatred for India, there has been no major war in South Asia since 1971. Indeed, between 1971 and the 1980s, the region enjoyed a period of lasting peace. This peace was based on overwhelming Indian conventional superiority but the same forced Pakistan's decision makers to foment terrorism in India's, first in Punjab and then in Kashmir, devising a strategy of a well-funded, carefully orchestrated, religiously motivated extortion racket or what General Zia termed as '*bleed by thousand cuts*'.[25] General Zia was the brain behind OP TUPAC,[26] aimed at diverting India's attention from conventional capability development and embroil the Indian armed forces in sub-conventional warfare of counter terrorism and anti-infiltration operations. The roots of Operation Tupac can be traced back to 1987, when India conducted 'Operation Brasstacks', a large-scale military exercise near the Rajasthan border. The primary objectives of Operation Tupac included: Phase 1: initiate low-level insurgency by infiltrating militants into J&K, targeting communication networks, and subverting local institutions. Phase 2: exert direct pressure along the Line of Control (LoC) through sabotage and infiltration, aiming to disrupt Indian military operations. Phase 3: mobilize religious sentiments to escalate the insurgency into a full-scale jihad, with the ultimate goal of integrating J&K into Pakistan.[27]

The incipient hatred forced Pakistan to develop nuclear capabilities, with the famous quote of Zulfikar Ali Bhutto,[28] the PM of Pakistan, "If India builds the bomb, we will eat grass or leaves, even go hungry, but we will get one of our own. We have no alternative." Thus, Indian conventional superiority has been countered by the nuclear threat even at the cost of the economic doldrums Pakistan brought upon itself. Pakistan holds its nuclear weapons as the ultimate guarantor of national survival and considers them as its most precious strategic asset. The military leadership is extremely conscious of its value as the ultimate guarantor of the nation's existence as a sovereign entity. This is evident in the writings of Gen. Mirza Aslam Beg. In an article appropriately titled "Pakistan's Nuclear Imperatives," he wrote, "Some safety against extinction is the inalienable right of an individual or a nation. Oxygen is basic to life, and one does not debate its desirability; nuclear deterrence has assumed that life-saving property for Pakistan."[29] Hatred of India is the raison d'etre of Pakistan's nuclear weapons. Its nuclear doctrine and strategy is wholly and solely India-centric, designed to address perceived conventional and nuclear threats from India.[30] Consequently, the nature and function of the Pakistani nuclear deterrent (including delivery mechanisms), as also its rules of employment and deployment, are all tailored to meet this single requirement. And, from this lone 'Brahmastra' in its repertoire of military capabilities, the Pakistan Army, given the nature of the system of governance in the country, expects to reap a rich harvest of military and political objectives.[31]

This inimical India rhetoric has allowed the Pakistan Army to maintain a stranglehold on the Pakistani budget. Pakistan's proposed defence allocation for 2025–26 stands at Rs. 2,281 billion, a Rs. 159 billion increase from the current fiscal year's Rs. 2,122 billion (USD 7.62 billion).[32] This increase, despite Pakistan grappling with economic challenges including double-digit inflation and a national budget where Rs. 9 trillion is earmarked for interest payments, indicates the growing defence budget increases with each passing year. As per the Pakistani media, the budget prioritizes immediate security needs, focusing on counter-terrorism (which mostly means operations against the Tehreek-e-Taliban and Baloch groups), border security, and military readiness. An additional USD 1.44 billion is allocated to the Armed Forces Development Programme (AFDP), supporting modernization efforts, including acquisitions like J-35 stealth jets and JF-17 Thunder aircraft through partnerships with China.[33] Despite fiscal constraints, defence remains a top priority, consuming approximately 2.8 per cent of Pakistan's GDP, a higher share than many regional peers. Nobody is allowed to protest against this rise inside Pakistan. In contrast, Pakistan allocated only 1.77 per cent of its GDP on education in 2024[34] clearly indicating the control the Pakistan Army wields, creating a paranoia in the state and the people about an 'Inimical India'.

Martial Race Complex

The first two commanders-in-chief of the Pakistan military were British[35] and at the time of independence there were 120 British officers serving in the Pakistan military in high ranks. General Sir Douglas Gracey was at the forefront of pronouncing a preference for martial race units.[36] This preference took deep root in the newly-formed Pakistan military officers' corps who were from Punjab or Pashtun origins. The changes in the recruitment policy of the Pakistan military were only a matter of carving the requirement between Pashtuns and Punjabis with no mention of the majority population, that is, the Bengalis of East Pakistan or that of other ethnicities. The perceived threat from India forced the Pakistan military to maintain 65 to 75 per cent of the military in the 1950s and 60s from the same areas of Punjab where the British formerly used to recruit (Fig. 5).[37] The martial race complex was further accentuated by the perceptible infallibility of an 'Islamic warrior'. The martial myth of wars fought under Prophet Mohammad was used to eulogize the spirit and capability of warriors fighting under the banner of Islam.[38] This vitriolic mix of a martial race complex and Islamic supremacy precipitated actions and responses which at times were not militarily prudent and at other times led to acts of unbridled valour and bravery.

The Punjabi and Pashtun officers provided a receptive audience to the British officers who were so enamoured with the idea of a martial race. This was the confirmation they sought for their self-existent belief of exceptionalism and elitism which was also inculcated in the new cadre of officers being trained at the PMA. The Pakistan officers' corps was indoctrinated by British officers to define themselves by religion and ethnicity and they took on the mantle of Islamic ghazis and saviours of the new Muslim homeland. The Pakistan military believed that a 'man on man' basis, they were much better than the Indian Army; the Hindus had connived with Lord Mountbatten to give the Pakistan military a raw deal and handicap them with respect to resources, assets and organizational structures. The Pakistan military also claimed that troops being repatriated on Partition were disarmed to reduce their combat potential.[39] According to a modern historian, Jeffrey Greenhut, on military history, "The martial race theory had an elegant symmetry. Indians who were intelligent and educated were defined as cowards, while those defined as brave were uneducated and backward." According to Amiya Samanta, the martial race was chosen from people of mercenary spirit (a soldier who fights for any group or country that will pay him), as these groups lacked nationalism as a trait. British-trained Indian soldiers were among those who had rebelled in 1857 and, thereafter, the Bengal army abandoned or diminished its recruitment of soldiers who came from the catchment area and enacted a new recruitment policy that favoured castes whose members had remained loyal to the British Empire.

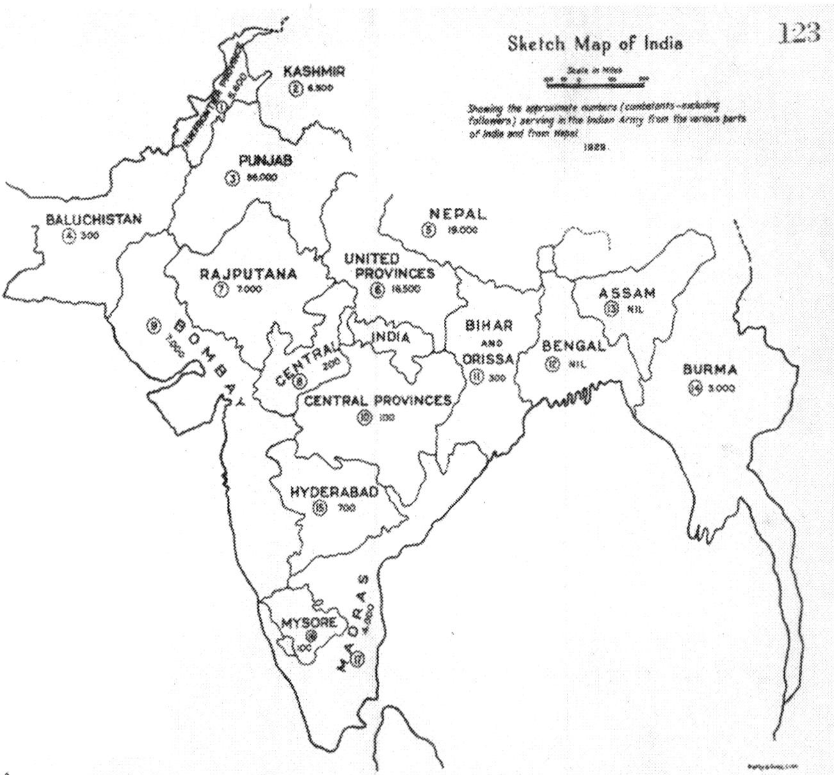

Fig. 6: Map Showing Recruitment of Army: 1929[40]

Within Punjab, only Sikhs and Punjabi Muslims were considered the martial classes and the Dogras and Hindu Jats were less preferred. Within the Sikh regiments, only those belonging to the dominant peasant Jat caste and adhering to the Khalsa creed were ideal recruits.[41] For instance, army recruitment for the year 1914-1918 had one per cent of combatant recruits from Bengal and 7.5 per cent from Madras while Punjab alone provided more than 50 per cent of the combatants.[42] A large chunk of recruitment from the Salt Range (the districts of Jhelum,

Rawalpindi, and Attock) was suggestive of the fact that there was a linkage between agriculture and the warrior ethos. The peasants and agriculturalists of this region were granted lands and allotted plots in the canal colonies as a reward for their military service and loyalty. The 'martial race' model had a smooth transition into the post-independence era and advantaged the dominant ethnicities. It left Bengalis from East Pakistan bereft of any representation in the army, despite being a major province. This became a source of tensions between the state and provinces. The myth continued to play a significant role in the military and advantaged the dominant ethnicities, who were drawn from these economically productive areas. The biases that came with the myth left Bengalis from East Pakistan bereft of any representation in the army, despite being a major province. Punjab province with 25 per cent of the population had 72 per cent representation in the army, whereas the East Bengal province with 55 per cent of the population had almost no representation in 1947. Steven Wilkinson in his recent book, *Army and Nation*, argues that Punjab (43%) and NWFP (14%) dominated the armoured corps, the elite of the elite Pakistan Army, in the post-Partition period. The armoured corps had no Muslims from Sindh, Baluchistan or Bengal, which, Wilkinson argues, accounted for around 70 per cent of the new state's population. This was also manifested in the composition of the officer corps in 1955, in which only 10 per cent of Bengalis were recruited in the air force and less than 1 per cent in the army.[43] It was also in the interest of the dominant ethnicities to maintain the status quo because of the privileges attached to the military ranks. This has been a cause of deep resentment amongst the Sindhis and Balochis and has manifested in the form of ethno-nationalist movements. Article 39 of the 1973 Constitution of Pakistan observes that the 'state shall enable people from all parts of Pakistan to participate in the armed forces of Pakistan.'[44]

Pakistan is a state that aspires to be modern. However, at a notional level, such modernity is an impossible, given the deeply entrenched tradition of a martial race. Pakistan continues to implement recruitment policies of the British era and prospects for change are bleak. Pakistan's strategic culture goes against the very notion of modern national armies, central to any modern bureaucratic state. The first opportunity to test the validity of their hypothesis of martial superiority was the 'Lashkars' in 1948. Officers being trained in the PMA took leave of absence to lead the Lashkars.[45] This myth of supremacy was key to the officers' actions. These tales became part of the syllabi at the PMA in the years to come. Henry Kissinger when interacting with General Yahya Khan asked him about the conventional asymmetry of Indians. The answer he received was the historic superiority of Muslim warriors.[46] This brazen complex has often led Pakistan to plan operations not based on critical analysis but on a false sense of bravado, visible both during OP GIBRALTAR and OP KOH-E-PAYMA.[47] The approach to military duties based on an interpretation of Islam to a point where military doctrine is subservient to Islam created a false sense of supremacy.

Islam under Threat

The alleged reticence of Indians during Partition to allow the Pakistan military the resources and assets translated into a larger Hindu conspiracy to target Islam. This thought was further exacerbated by police action in Hyderabad, Junagarh and of course Kashmir. Defining the idea of Pakistan or 'Pakistaniyat'[48] for the Pakistan military became synonymous not with the concept of democracy and the constitution but Islam. The supposed loss of Kashmir despite the heroism of jihadi Lashkars became a key element of the Pakistan military's strategic culture. The role to defend Islam began with General Ayub Khan who took over the state to build a strong central government that would be reinforced by Islam.[49] In Ayub's autobiography, *Friends Not Masters*, he points out the most significant problem as "*India's inability to reconcile herself to our existence as a sovereign independent state. The leaders have a deep hatred for the Muslims.*

From the beginning, India was determined to make things difficult for us."[50] Under Ayub, the military and government undertook an exercise of myth and folklore to glorify the military.[51] While Ayub may have been the first to advocate a role of the military to protect the ideology of Pakistan, he started a chain reaction which was taken to a state of critical mass by General Zia who espoused the view that "*preservation of ideology and Islamic character of the country was as important as the security of geographical boundary.*"[52] Zia aimed at invoking the original social Islamic order that existed in the times of the Prophet. Zia replaced the motto of the military coined by Jinnah (Faith, Unity & Discipline) with *Imam, Taqwa, Jihad-fi-Sabilillah* (Faith, Piety, Holy War in the name of God).[53]

The sequestering of East Pakistan into Bangladesh by India in 1971 was a strategic shock which the Pakistani armed forces are yet to recover from. On the issue of developing a narrative, the Pakistan Army has apportioned the blame of the debacle to the politicians but internally it is still smarting from the bloody nose it got. As Pakistan approached war with India in 1971, the Americans were surprised at the arrogance and naiveteì of the Pakistani army generals' belief in their martial race identity and Islamic exceptionalism to rescue them from their developing debacle. The impact of the loss of the war was a strategic shock for the army that caused it to question both its leadership and culture. A strategic shock or a strategic surprise may be explained as believing those events, if they occur, would make a big difference to the futurc, forcc decision makers to challenge their own assumptions of how the world works, and require hard choices today.[54] In particular, the loss ignited a belief that attributed blame to a great degree on the moral turpitude of the senior officer corps. These officers came to be thought of as irreligious and slavish followers of the inherited culture from the British Indian Army. In rowdy scenes after the war, younger officers distinctly saw the non-religiosity of their officers as a major factor in the humiliating loss to India. Since then and till date, any action by India conforms to the military's perception of Islam under threat which has further been accentuated by the hyper-nationalism on display in India. Yahya Khan had branded the Mukti Bahini as 'Kafirs' against which the military was waging jihad. Brigadier Javed Hasan, who retired as Lieutenant General, published *India: A Study in Profile,* while at FORAD[55] which is compulsory reading for the Command & Staff College and the National Defence University. It is peppered with disparaging remarks against the Indian Army being solely a Hindu force providing heft to the argument of jihad when Islam is under threat.

The Quranic Concept of War, a book by Brigadier S. K. Malik of the Pakistan Army, provides readers with unrivalled insight. It states, "The most glorious word in the vocabulary of Islam is *Jehad,* a word which is untranslatable in English but, broadly speaking, means striving, struggling, trying to advance the Divine causes or purposes." He introduces a somewhat cryptic concept when he explains man's role in a 'Quranic setting' as energetically combating forces of evil or what may be called, 'counter-initiatory' forces which are at war with the harmony and purpose of life on earth.[56] For the true Muslin, the harmony and purpose in life are only possible through man's ultimate submission to God's will so that all will come to know, recognize, and profess Mohammed as the Prophet of God. Man must recognize the last days and acknowledge *tawhid,* the oneness of God.[57] The classic dualism of Islamic theology believes that the world is a place of struggle between good and evil, between right and wrong, between *Haq* and *Na-Haq* (truth and untruth) and between *halal* and *haram* (legitimate and forbidden). The *jihad* doctrine developed for the Pakistan Army places *jihad* in the context of communal obligation, a controversial formulation.

As per Brigadier Malik, when a believer sees that someone is trying to obstruct another believer from travelling the road that leads to God, the spirit of *jihad* requires that such a man who is imposing obstacles should be prevented from doing so and the obstacles placed by him should also be removed, so that mankind may be freely able to negotiate its own path that leads to Heaven. To do otherwise, "by not striving to clear or straighten the path, we [Muslims] become passive spectators of the counter-initiatory forces imposing a blockade in the way of those who mean to keep their faith with God.[58] This viewpoint appears to reflect the classic, collective duty in the *jihad* doctrine of the Pakistan Army to defend the Islamic community of Pakistan from threats by non-believers, the concept of defensive *jihad against India*. This formulation would appear to turn the concept of defence on its head. To the extent that a Muslim may proclaim Islam and proselytize, or Islam, as a faith, seeks to extend its invitation and reach, initiate its advance, but is unable to do so, then that represents an overt threat justifying a defensive *jihad*.

Military Elitism

Despite its recurrent praetorianism and interference in national politics, the rules within the armed forces seem to be generally followed, with limited factionalism and consistent promotion pathways. There is the stark contrast between this rational-bureaucratic organization and other political militaries. Internal bureaucratic discipline, fused with the continued cooperation of elites *even after they retire,* is crucial to the military's professional cohesion and its high levels of power within Pakistani society. This distinctive combination has allowed the Pakistan Army remarkable influence over key areas of national policy, even when it does not directly rule the country. Standard theories of military professionalism and praetorianism may miss the crucial coexistence of internal professionalism and external politicization. The elitism within the Pakistan Army is further stratified with respect to regions, ethnicity, religion and even arms and services. The manifestations of the societal norms in the Pakistan Army can be easily identified by the fact that of the officers who became corps commanders since 2004, 61 per cent are from Punjab, 18 per cent from KPK, and 7 per cent from Sindh.[59] This suggests a tilt towards Punjab and continued Sindhi under-representation at the highest levels of the military, which aligns with society as well that showed Sindhi under-representation and over-representation from KPK in recruitment. They identify something of an increase over time from Sindh, however, which may eventually translate into representation in the military elite. The Pakistan Army is dominated by the infantry; 66 per cent are from the infantry, 15 per cent from the armoured corps, 14 per cent from the artillery, and less than 5 per cent from the Corps of Engineers and Air Defence.[60]

The Pakistan Army is a highly bureaucratic organization with quite a routinized, institutionalized and professionally-relevant trajectory to the top. There does not appear to be the wild factionalism, personalization or weak institutionalization of some other highly political militaries. Though the very top of the ladder, selection to corps commander, has room for personal preferences with the army chief enjoying considerable latitude, most rungs below the highest echelon follow a systematic and predictable path. Employing a routinized meritocratic system has the benefit of minimizing internal disagreements and grievances, an important consideration for an organization intensely conscious of its public image as unified and cohesive. However, the army is changing in ways that make the future hard to predict. The feudal elites no longer send their sons to the army. Instead, they despatch them to universities in the West and into banking or business. This has broken the link between the civilian elite and the army. Instead, army officers are now from the lower middle class and even more humble backgrounds. They are not products of private schools but the education system predicated on madrassas and government schools they are less in awe of the tiny ruling class in Pakistan and its Westernised habits including democracy and would prefer *sharia*. They are trained to be hostile to India, but they are also wary of being sucked too deeply into China's orbit. President Musharraf experienced significant opposition from his corps commanders but the COASs in the recent past are becoming less 'first among equals' and more dictatorial, be it General Bajwa or the present incumbent, General Munir. The army is more unpopular inside Pakistan than at any time since 1947.

Lust for Power

General Ayub Khan initiated the Pakistan military to the psychotropic addiction of power which, over a period under General Zia, General Musharraf and even General Kayani has calcified into the strategic culture of the Pakistan military.[61]

Over a period, Pakistani democratic structures like the judiciary, executive and media have become more dysfunctional, and the Pakistan military has become more entrenched in the governance of the nation-state. It is pertinent to mention here that this enhanced influence of the Pakistan military in the affairs of the state take place with the acquiescence and connivance of other stake holders and with tacit approval of the populace which provides the system legitimacy. During various direct or indirect interferences by the military, it has strengthened its hold over economic installations, cultivated a cabal of bureaucrats, industry, media, and feudal elites, eroded the capacity and capability of the political system and attenuated the opposition to military intervention.

To cement the power of the military in politics, General Musharraf took two instrumental steps. First, he reinstated Article 58(2)(b) and second, he created the NSC. These "sanctified the military's control of politics." By Article 58(2)(b) the President can disband the government. This article has been removed and added to the constitution numerous times; however, the military elites seek solace from its presence. The NSC mutated the role of the military to an organization that had equal footing with the civilian and political sectors of the country. The IRI conducted a poll in Pakistan in 2009[62] which indicated public acceptance of the Pakistan military as the final answer to their vicissitudes. Even the Pakistan media which prima facie is vibrant and independent withdraws into a shell of self-censorship and partisan subservience to the ISPR and the Pakistan military.

The judiciary also is a tool of the Pakistan military which was very much visible in the form of a judicial coup where General Kayani's support to the Chief Justice of Pakistan and the lawyers' movement in 2007 against Musharraf led to his final resignation as President of Pakistan.[63] Kayani's non-interference in matters of the state and refusal to support President Zardari came to be known as the 'Kayani Model'[64] and led to grant of extension to General Kayani in 2010 by PM Geelani whose powers were restored by passing of the 18th Amendment by the Pakistan Assembly.[65] General Bajwa however relapsed into the trap of direct machinations so much so that the famous Bajwa Doctrine[66] was not a commentary on the military as a vector of national power but other vectors as well. Imran Khan's meteoric rise and fall can be attributed to his fallout with the military hierarchy which ended up designating him a 'national security threat'.[67] General Bajwa's insinuations were also visible in the foreign policy narrative of Pakistan wherein he visited the USA[68] to develop a rapprochement and interactions with China[69] to secure financial doles; this revealed the military control over the economy. The present COAS, General Asim Munir, has assured the nation that he would keep the military out of the political morass the nation is presently in.[70] The tiered control of the SIFC is indicative of the Munir Doctrine influence on the governance and economic policy of the nation.

In the second edition of the book, *Military Inc.*, Ayesha Siddiqa has added a new chapter on the military's expanding control over the Pakistani media as part of the lust of power to control all the elements of society. The army has very systematically encouraged an armed forces biased narrative and has also developed a new nationalist discourse to keep its institution relevant not only for the state but for society as well. With the help of the media, the Deep State has managed to widely spread the image of a nationalist soldier, who is highly professional, yet upholds the religious values of Islam. The Pakistan military has developed an extensive communications structure and a strategy to engage with formal civil society and with society at large. There are several tiers of engagement. The most obvious is the ISPR (Inter-Services Public Relations) that was originally formed in the early years after the independence of the country in order to disseminate information regarding military affairs. Over the years, it has evolved, finally resulting in the position of the Director-General ISPR being upgraded from a colonel to the rank of a Lt. General.[71] This could also be interpreted as part of Milbus that is creating positions for military personnel. However, there were obvious institutional reasons for doing so, such as guiding the process of discourse generation and its implementation. The ISPR's upgrade involved financing and supporting the local film industry, theatre and an extensive radio network.

Since 2007, the ISPR has developed separate units to engage with radio, television and other forms of media. As far as its main role of interacting with journalists is concerned, it has even enhanced its role from just providing information, to courting and influencing journalists. The head of the ISPR under Kayani was even known to send birthday cakes to elite journalists. However, the agency was also known for intimidation such as directing television channels regarding their choice of news-programme anchors, and in certain cases, even their choice of guests. The role of influencing public opinion was expanded even more in 2010 and 2011 when the ISPR established a private radio network, '96 International Radio Network'[72] which was the second largest after the state-run Pakistan Broadcasting Corporation (PBC). The company has continued to operate illegally since September 2011 when the Director-General PBC declined permission to set up this company as an independent subsidiary of the state-run radio company. The human-rights activist and lawyer, Asma Jahangir, challenged the ISPR's role in the Supreme Court asking the government to disclose the number of channels that the military PR agency ran.[73] In 2016, a major step was taken by making efforts to rebuild the weak and fledgling industry that could not compete with Bollywood. It is believed that the

ISPR support to filmmakers is limited to providing logistic support. Such support includes providing manpower and even camera units, which, according to sources in the film industry, were imported by the PR agency. Brigadier-ranking officers in uniform who were present during the meetings instructed film industry stakeholders to make films that did not challenge national interest, which translated as supporting a narrative that challenged the traditional elite, painted the military in bright colours, portrayed India as an enemy and followed the army line on sensitive issues.[74] Subsequently, films such as *Waar*[75] produced in 2013 blamed India for terrorism inside the country and painted the military as a saviour. It also set the tone in terms of spreading the security establishment's perspective on the highly divisive issue of the construction of the Kalabagh Dam, presenting any opposition to the idea as propaganda by India. Another film, *Maalik*, produced in 2016, built the idea of vigilante justice by a group of retired army officers.[76]

While the ISPR may be the most overt form of the army's interaction with the media and civil society, there are other levels of engagement, such as the ISI's media wing. The intelligence agency independently sought both domestic and international journalists and academics to inform them or convert them to the military's point of view. Providing these people with the military's perspective during the war on terror was essential from two standpoints. First, to provide an army-sympathetic version that countered the accusation of Pakistan military's collusion with the Taliban and other terrorist groups like the Lashkar-e-Taiyba (LeT) accused of carrying out attacks in Mumbai, India, in 2008. Such publicity was critical to negotiate relations with the USA. Second, to convince foreign experts regarding the military's superior capabilities and posit it as the most performing institution of the state. But the ISI's role was not limited to soft diplomacy. Often, fingers were pointed at it for engaging in coercive treatment of journalists. The killing of the journalist, Saleem Shahzad,[77] or the torture of another journalist, Umer

Cheema,[78] were attributed to the intelligence agency. Conscious of psy-ops as a new trend in warfare, the ISI also created a separate cyber-security wing,[79] with the purpose of not just securing military or state data, but also to influence trends on social media, hack websites and mine the data of enemy states. The message, spread through the popular media site Facebook, used the lyrics from a Nancy Sinatra song to lighten the real missive that politicians of questionable reputation such as Asif Ali Zardari and Altaf Hussain would be thrashed by the army. Such propaganda seems to have caught on, especially among the growing extended middle class in the country that began to believe in this narrative. The fact that this middle class was unable to push out these politicians through the electoral process has helped to build the military's image even further as a possible saviour. Despite adopting such tactics, the military's PR machinery could not effectively gag social media that is far more independent than traditional forms of the media in most countries. In August 2016, the Pakistan National Assembly (PNA) passed a controversial cyber security bill called the Prevention of Electronic Crime Bill 2015[80] that civil society and human-rights activists believe is regressive in content and could result in the state curbing dissent. Any criticism of the country, the judiciary, religion and armed forces is liable to punishment.

A bid to control cyber space seemed to be part of a larger agenda to capture discourse formulation, which was one of the primary goals of the military's PR exercise. This is also one of the reasons why the ISI and its officer cadre take an interest in engaging with young students and scholars in national and foreign universities from Pakistan or working on it. For instance, in the UK, which is a major hub of Pakistani students both from the country and the Diaspora, the ISI officer in the High Commission was observed influencing student activities in the university. In 2009 and 2010, the agency even tried to plant a conglomerate of Pakistani student societies around British universities.[81] In another instance in 2014, the Pakistan Society at Oxford

University was forced to invite military-friendly journalists to its event.[82] In a similar fashion, its sister organization, the ISPR sought out non-Pakistani, usually Anglo-Saxon scholars, to write military-friendly books. Furthermore, during Kayani's era, the ISI allegedly established a fund to finance scholars in American think-tanks.[83] This was to generate sympathy for Pakistan among American policy makers and opinion makers. A bigger programme was launched in the country because of which there was a proliferation of think-tanks[84] in the capital Islamabad. Although these are private entities, the perspective followed on national security does not deviate from the military's point of view.

The lust for power of the Pakistan military also translates into the post-retirement employment of military elite. Kings College, London, conducted a study on Pakistan military elites[85] which indicates that there is a clearly institutionalized transmission belt that shifts retired elites into military-owned foundations and corporations, specific posts in the civil

Position	1978-88	1989-1998	1999-2007	2008-2017
Fauji Company	1 (5)	9 (24)	9 (23)	14 (33)
Province Governor	5 (26)	2 (5)	3 (7.5)	0
Federal Govt. Minister	3 (16)	3 (8)	2 (5)	1 (2)
Ambassador	4 (21)	0	4 (10)	4 (9.5)
Head of Sports Organization	0	3 (8)	4 (10)	3 (7)
Head/Founder/Member of School or NGO	1 (5)	5 (13)	8 (20)	5 (12)
Electoral Politics	0	0	2 (5)	0
Academic/Think tank	0	6 (16)	1 (2.5)	2 (5)
Defence Secretary	0	1 (3)	1 (2.5)	5 (12)
Head of Fed. Govt. Agency	0	3 (8)	3 (7.5)	1 (2)
Private Company	1 (5)	1 (3)	1 (2.5)	0
Head of Provincial Govt. Agency	1 (5)	0	1 (2.5)	3 (7)
Other	3 (15)	6 (13)	1 (2.5)	4 (9.5)
Total	19	38	40	42

Fig. 7: First Retirement Roles by Period (percentage in parentheses)[86]

government, and other positions of real and/or symbolic authority. These positions of influence, in addition to generous pensions and other benefits, provide powerful incentives to toe the organizational line and keep control over civil organization. Importantly, these 'off-ramps' are centrally controlled by GHQ. During the study, post-retirement avenues of corps commanders from independence to 2017 was tabulated (Fig. 7).

Conclusion

The impact of Partition along with the propagation of beliefs in a martial race, cohered with the impact of the war (1947–48) into a mythology of the potential danger that a Hindu India presented to Islam, was a cry to the faithful to join the battle against the Indians. The convergence of these elements led to the foundation of a strategic culture derived from shared hardships, disasters, and a call to Islam. The strategic culture founded during independence in 1947 has evolved with new vistas and hues to the contours in its internal and geostrategic relationships. That this strategic culture is dexterous and dynamic, attuned to realism to ensure the survival of the Pakistani state, are deliberated upon in the subsequent chapter.

NOTES

1 Gill, Anila. "Inhabiting a Moth-Eaten Method." *Framework: The Journal of Cinema and Media* 63, no. 1 (2022): 77-81. https://doi.org/10.1353/frm.2022.a875877.
2 Briskey, Mark. "The Foundations of Pakistan's Strategic Culture: Fears of an Irredentist India, Muslim Identity, Martial Race, and Political Realism." *Journal of Advanced Military Studies* 13 (2022): 130-152. muse.jhu.edu/article/851423.
3 Schofield Carey, Inside the Pakistan Army: A Woman's Experience on the Frontline of the War on Terror. Pentagon Security International, 2011, p. 45.
4 Ibid, p. 44.
5 Coughley Brian, A History of Pakistan Army, Wars and Insurrections (Third Edition), Oxford University Press, Karachi, 2006, p. 3.
6 https://content.time.com/time/subscriber/article/0,33009,815599,00.html accessed on 04 Feb 22.
7 Cohen, Stephen. P. (2004). *The Idea of Pakistan*. Brookings Institution Press. Pg 54.
8 Maj Gen Shahid Hamid, Early Years of Pakistan: Including the Period from

Aug 47 to 1949, Ferozesons, Lahore 1993, pp. 41-50.
9 Schofield, p. 19.
10 https://knowindia.india.gov.in/national-identity-elements/national-song.php accessed on 12 Apr 24.
11 Cohen Stephen Philip, India, Pakistan and Kashmir, The Brookings Institution, Presented at the University of Texas, December 2001.https://www.brookings.edu/wp-content/uploads/2016/06/cohens20011201.pdf accessed on 24 May 24.
12 Khan Feroze Hassan, The Durand Line: Tribal Politics & Pak Afghan Relations, Stanford University Press, 2014, p. 148.
13 Coughley, p. 39.
14 https://www.dawn.com/news/1213461 accessed on 23 Mar 23.
15 Schofield, p. 58.
16 Wahab Shaista, Brief History of Afghanistan, Youngerman, 2007, ISBN 978-0-8160-5761-0.
17 Sharma, Pankaj Kumar. "Conflict Over Water Between India and Pakistan: Fear and Hopes?" *The Indian Journal of Political Science* 73, no. 1 (2012): 133–40. http://www.jstor.org/stable/41856568.
18 Malik Anas, Pol Survival in Pak: Beyond Ideology, Taylor & Francis, 2010, p. 42.
19 http://www.columbia.edu/itc/mealac/pritchett/ooislamlinks/txt_jinnah_assembly_1947.html accessed on 21 Mar 23.
20 Akhtar Safir, Pakistan Since Independence; The Political Role of Ulema, PhD Dissertation, University of York, 1989, p. 234.
21 https://www.uscirf.gov/sites/default/files/2011%20Annual%20Report.pdf accessed on 24 May 24. Pg 118. The education system of Pakistan breeds contempt and hatred for all other religions and also blames India for all the travails of Pakistan in history and at present as well.
22 https://www.orfonline.org/research/story-of-saltoro-from-ababeel-to-meghdoot accessed on 12 Jan 25.
23 https://swarajyamag.com/defence/former-chief-general-s-padmanabhan-who-led-the-indian-army-in-the-crucial-operation-parakram-against-pakistan accessed on 12 Jan 25.
24 https://www.reuters.com/world/asia-pacific/indias-military-response-previous-attacks-kashmir-blamed-pakistan-2025-05-01/ accessed on 01 May 25.
25 https://economictimes.indiatimes.com/news/defence/inside-operation-tupac-pakistans-secret-project-to-burn-kashmir/articleshow/120865333.cms?from=mdr accessed on 03 May 25.
26 Lekshmi Parameswaran, Pakistan's Designs to Destabilise India, India Policy Foundation, D-51, Hauz Khas, New Delhi, Feb 2020, pp. 8-10.
27 Liza Gupta, (2022). 1990 Kashmir Insurgency: An analysis of Geo-Political Security Situation. OP Jindal Global University.
28 https://timesofindia.indiatimes.com/world/pakistan/50-years-ago-pakistan-said-itll-eat-grass-to-get-its-own-bomb-its-doing-just-that/articleshow/92797530.cms accessed on 01 May 25.

29 Gen. Mirza Aslam Beg, "Pakistan's Nuclear Imperatives," National Development and Security, vol.3, no.10, November 1994, pp. 29-41.

30 Manpreet Sethi, Pakistan's Nuclear Doctrine and Strategy, *Air Power Journal*, Vol. 2, No. 3 Monsoon 2007 (July-September), Centre for Air Power Studies, New Delhi, pp. 77-78.

31 Peter Lavoy in his essay on Pakistan's nuclear doctrine has listed eight separate "uses" for Pakistan's nuclear weapons, four being specific to India, viz (i) last resort weapons to prevent military defeat or loss of territory; (ii) deterrent to conventional military attack; (iii) facilitators of low-intensity conflict; and (iv) tools to internationalise the Kashmir issue. See Rafiq Dossani, Henry S. Rowen, Prospects for Peace in South Asia (Stanford: Stanford University Press, 2005).

32 https://resonantnews.com/2025/04/16/pakistan-plans-to-increase-defense-spending-by-7-5/ accessed on 01 May 25.

33 Ibid.

34 https://www.paradigmshift.com.pk/education-budget/ accessed on 01 May 25.

35 https://www.dawn.com/news/1722817 accessed on 31 Jan 24.

36 McCullough, Robin James Fitch, Imperial Influence of Post-Colonial Indian Army 1945-1953, University of Vermont, 2017. p. 23.

37 Air Chief Marshall Muhammad Asghar Khan, 'Tareekh say kuch nahin sikha-Siyyasat aur Afwaj-e-Pakistan' (We learnt nothing from history, Politics and Pakistan Army) An autobiography, (Karachi: Oxford University Press, 2005), p. 21.

38 Hayward, Joel. The Warrior Prophet: Muhammad and War, Swansea, UKClaritas Books, 2022, p. 18.

39 Brig MAH Ansari, Col Mehboob Elahi, History of Pak Army Ord Corps 1947-92, Ferozesons, Rawalpindi, 1993, pp. 89-90.

40 Reports from Commissioners, Inspectors, and Others: [Hereafter RCIO] Ten Volumes. Vol. 4. East India Continued. Session: June 1929-August 1930, p. 96.

41 Tan Tai Yong, The Garrison State, SAGE publications, New Delhi, 2005, pp. 71-72.

42 Steven Wilkinson, Army and Nation, Permanent Black, Ranikhet, 2015, p. 50.

43 C. Christine Fair and Shuja Nawaz, "The Changing Pakistan Army Officer Corps", Journal of Strategic Studies, Vol. 34, No. 1, February, 2011, p. 76.

44 Ayesha Siddiqa, Pakistan Military-Ethnic balance in the Armed Forces and problems of Federalism, Manekshaw Paper, Centre for Land Warfare Studies, No. 39, 2013, p. 14.

45 Brig ZA Khan, The Way It Was: Inside the Pak Army, Ahbab Printers, Karachi, 1998, p. 44.

46 Kissinger Henry, The White House Years, Holder & Stoughton, 1979, p. 861.

47 https://sundayguardianlive.com/news/23-years-kargil-war-op-vijay-prevailed-op-koh-paima, published on 23 Jun 22 accessed on 23 Mar 23.

48 J MoosviAbbas, A Muddled Identity, Pak Institute of Development, https://pide.org.pk.

49 Fair Christine, Fighting to the End: The Pak Army's Way of War, Johnson Press, India, 2014, p. 73.

50 Khan MA, Friends Not Masters, Mr Books, Islamabad, reprint 2006, p. 135.
51 Rizvi Hassan Askari, The Military& Politics in Pak; 1947-1997, Sang-e-Mell Publishers, 2006, p. 256.
52 Kukreja Veena, Contemporary Pak; Pol Processes, Conflicts and Crises, New Delhi, 2003, Sage Publications.
53 Fair Christine, Fighting to the End: The Pak Army's Way of War, Johnson Press, India, 2014, p. 76.
54 A strategic shock may also be explained as an event that has an important impact onthe country and/or stretches conventional wisdom with fundamental implications, or as Freier explains more informally, "a game changing event that changes the nature of the game." Freier, Known Unknowns, pp. 4–5.
55 Fair Christine, Fighting to the End: The Pak Army's Way of War, Johnson Press, India, 2014, p. 100.
56 David Cook, *Understanding Jihad*, (Berkeley: Univ. of California Press, 2005). There isapproximately 1,400 years of *jihad* scholarship beginning with Mohammed and his militarycampaigns. Classical approaches to *jihad* as described by Mohammed's successors, Abu Bakr forexample, and the challenges presented by the struggles of succession to Mohammed.
57 Brigadier S. K. Malik, *The Quranic Concept of War* (Lahore, Pakistan: Associated Printers,1979). Preface.
58 Ibid, p. 1.
59 P Staniland, A Naseemullah & A Butt (2018). Pakistan's Military Elite. *Journal of Strategic Studies*, *43*(1), 74–103. https://doi.org/10.1080/01402390.2018.1497487.
60 Ibid.
61 Fair Christine, Why the Pak Army is here to Stay: Prospects for Civil Governance. Paper presented by the author during Brookings Institute Conference on 'The Future of Pak', May 2010. p. 2.
62 It asked people the question; "Under what circumstances should the military be able to take over power?" 69% respondents voted in favour of "in an emergency" and seven percent voted for "whenever it wants."
63 Human Rights Watch, Destroying Legality, Pakistan's Crackdown on Lawyers and Judges, New York, HRW, 2007, International Affairs, p. 87.
64 The Pakistan Military in this model was to be invisible yet omnipresent, fully aware and responding through precise and effective stimuli, during a crisis. Kayani Model' was effective in retaining control of military over the civilian government surreptitiously. https://www.nytimes.com/2009/03/17/world/asia/17pstan.html accessed on 21 Jun 24.
65 https://www.scribd.com/doc/30269950/18th-ammendment-in-the-constitution-of-pakistan-complete-text accessed on 30 Mar 23.
66 https://rusi.org/explore-our-research/publications/rusi-newsbrief/bajwa-doctrine-pakistani-military-has-done-more-enough accessed on 28 Mar 23.
67 https://www.tbsnews.net/worl/ex-army-chief-says-imrans-ruling-was-threat-pakisan-583586 accessed on 29 Mar 23.
68 https://pakobserver.net/bajwas-visit-helps-maintain-a-visionary-pak-us-

reset-by-syed-qamar-afzal-rizvi/ accessed on 29 Mar 23.

69 https://www.brecorder.com/news/40180175 accessed on 29 Mar 23.

70 https://www.aninews.in/news/world/asia/pas-army-chief-asim-munir-maintains-to-not-interfere-in-politics20230309040809 accessed on 31 Mar 23.

71 https://caravanmagazine.in/vantage/military-pakistan-influences-countrys-media accessed on 05 May 25.

72 https://www.bbc.com/news/world-asia-18766713 accessed on 01 May 25.

73 https://www.dw.com/en/how-pakistans-military-uses-media-for-image-making/a-19335614 accessed on 01 May 25.

74 Siddiqa, Ayesha. (2016) 2016. *Military Inc.* 2nd ed. Pluto Press. https://www.perlego.com/book/664599/military-inc-inside-pakistans-military-economy-pdf.

75 https://economictimes.indiatimes.com/industry/media/entertainment/pakistan-movies-waar-the-film-on-real-life-terror-strike-raises-hopes-for-another-revival/articleshow/12049756.cms?from=mdr accessed on 23 Apr 25.

76 https://www.bbc.com/news/world-asia-36157115 accessed on 24 Apr 25.

77 https://www.amnesty.be/IMG/pdf/amnesty_-_attacks_on_journalists_pakistan_final.pdf accessed on 23 Apr 25.

78 Ibid.

79 https://issi.org.pk/wp-content/uploads/2022/09/4_Muhammad_N_Mirza_and_Muhammad_S_Akram_No-1_2022.pdf accessed on 24 Apr 25.

80 https://cscr.pk/explore/themes/social-issues/the-prevention-of-electronics-crimes-bill-2015/ accessed on 30 Apr 25.

81 Radical islam on UK campuses, AComprehensive List of Extremist Speakers at UK Universities, The Centre for Social Cohesion 2010, Clutha House, 10 Storey's Gate London, p. 4.

82 PervezHoodbhoy, "How the Pakistan Military Controls the Narrative Abroad." Dawn, January 10, 2015. https://www.dawn.com accessed on 21 Apr 25.

83 Fair, C. Christine. "Pakistan's War on Scholars." The Huffington Post, February 17, 2015. https://www.huffpost.com/entry/pakistans-war-onscholars_b_6695986. accessed on 11 Apr 25.

84 According to the 2020 Global Go To Think Tank Index Report by the University of Pennsylvania's Think Tanks and Civil Societies Program (TTCSP), Pakistan was home to 19 think tanks at that time.

85 Staniland P, Naseemullah, A, & Butt, A. (2020). Pakistan's military elite. Journal of Strategic Studies, 43 (1), 74-103. https://doi.org/10.1080/01402390.2018.1497487.

86 Ibid, p. 29.

Three

Societal Stressors

General

The birth of Pakistan in 1947 was the conversion of a myth or a figment of the imagination of a few in the Indian subcontinent. Hariri, the famous author of the book *Sapiens* says, "*Humans are special, because they inhabit an imagined world, created from their ideas which they construe as real.*"[1] Using this capability, humans have created stories that helped them to unite and collaborate in groups unlike any other animal. Pakistan was one such story, conceived by Chaudhary Rehmat Ali in 1933 at Cambridge.[2] This story galvanized the Muslim masses in the Indian subcontinent to rally against a perceived threat of marginalization and permanent subjugation as a minority. Once a myth calcifies, it defies logic, reason and history and so was the case with the idea of the Two-Nation Theory (TNT). Allama Iqbal, the national icon of Pakistan, had a prescriptive vaccine for the newly-born Pakistan,[3] one of valorisation of *jihad* and the confluence of democracy and theocracy into a *theodemocracy.*[4] The edicts of his idea were; one, no difference between temporal and spiritual; two, all laws had to be aligned to the Qur'an; and finally, all legislations for a modern society would be the fruition of the process of *ijtihad.*[5] While Pakistan was carved in the minds of an elite few, the fruition on ground had myriad challenges of trying to coalesce ethnicities and sects together into one whole.

Pakistan has emerged as a Muslim-majority state having more than 90 per cent of Muslim population. Jinnah had in 1948 at Dacca said, "If you want to build up yourself into a nation, for God's sake give up this provincialism and sectarianism."[6] These fractures still remain in society and have a domino effect on the Pakistan military as well; after all, the armed forces are a microcosm of society itself.

Sectarianism (Inter-Sect)

Jinnah had flip-flopped between secularism and Islamism creating an existential paradox but in Pakistan's first six years as a new state, the emergence of political organizations along sectarian lines was remote. The Shia community in Pakistan could not claim to be oppressed with many of the Muslim League's leaders being Shias, including Jinnah himself,[7] with successive Pakistani governments having a fair share of Shia ministers.[8] Despite occasional riots during the month of Muharram, most Shias in Pakistan did not feel discriminated against. General Zia's ascent as the most religious dictator led to the confluence of Islamization and securitization of the state. Zia announced in 1978 the primacy of the Nizam-e-Mustafa Tehreek and the Sunni Sharia's precedence over the constitution.[9] His allegiance to the Hanafi school of Sunni Islam manifested in the institution of *zakat*. The JeI's interaction with the state and military became stronger, much to the chagrin of the Shia community. The Tehrik-e-Nifaz-e-Fiqh-e-Jafaria (TNFJ) was formed in 1979[10] by Allama Jaffer Hussein as a defensive fail-safe to allay the fears of Shias of meeting the same fate as the Ahmadiyyas; of being declared non-Muslims. The agitation by Shias in 1980 precipitated an escapist response from General Zia. By exempting the Shias from paying *zakat* set both Shias and Sunnis on a collision course.

The rise and sustenance of the Salafi-inspired movement in Pakistan that sees all Shias as heretics to be targeted and destroyed occurs outside the dynamics of regime survival and is not a new phenomenon.[11] The Sipah-e-Sahaba's genesis in

Pakistan in the 1980s and its attacks on the Shia community was as much a result of a proxy war between Saudi Arabia and Iran[12] as also the weakening of Zia's stranglehold on power and his need for an organization to act as his henchman, supported and trained by Pakistan's Intelligence arm.[13] Zia sent out a directive to identify and weed out Shia officers[14] and at the same time the influence of the Salafi strain in the military grew manifold due to the close interaction between the Saudi royal army and the Pakistan military. "Until the late 1970s, mosques located in armed forces bases (i.e., Army, Air Force and Navy) were 90 per cent Ahle Sunnat Wal Jama't (Sufi), 8 per cent Deobandi, and zero per cent Salafi. Currently, 85 per cent of the mosques are Deobandi or Salafi, and less than 10 per cent are Ahle Sunnat Wal Jama't,"[15] a clear indicator of the shrinking space for sectarian tolerance within the military.

The Pakistan Army has been able to control the Shia-Sunni divide due to lack of militarization of Shia groups. The minority status of this group has ensured that they do not respond to the violence meted out to them in various parts of Pakistan but this may change after the fall of the Syrian regime of ousted President Asad.[16] Shias have so far been submissive and languished at the bottom of the food chain in both Pakistan and Afghanistan, but with the IRGC in Iran having mobilized recruits to fight the Islamic State in Syria,[17] Pakistani Shias joined the fight. On 24 July 2024, Pakistan's Religious Affairs Minister, Chaudhury Salik Hussain, told the Senate of Pakistan that around 50,000 Pakistani pilgrims visiting the Shi'ite holy sites in Iraq 'have vanished,' an admission that Iran has been recruiting Shi'ias from Pakistan.[18] This was a consequence of the IS campaign of destroying Shia holy shrines in Syria and Iraq. The 2013 rocket attack by the IS on the Sayeeda Zainab mosque in central Damascus, which destroyed the outer walls of the shrine of Zainab,[19] the sister of Imam Hussain and granddaughter of Mohammed, provided the catalyst; a new militant unit of Pakistani Shias, the Zainabiyoun Brigade, was raised with Iranian support. The Zainabiyoun

Brigade has been fighting in and around Damascus where scores of its fighters were supposedly killed while defending the shrine of Zainab.

Fig. 8: Zainab Brigade in Iraq[20]

When the Assad regime imploded in 24 December, one of many unanswered questions was what would happen to the large number of Afghan and Pakistani Shia fighters in Syria who are controlled by Iran's Islamic Revolutionary Guard Corps (IRGC) and brigaded under the Liwa Fatemiyoun and Liwa Zainabiyoun militias. Fatemiyoun and Zainabiyoun personnel have entered Iraq via al-Qaim and are being hosted by Qasim Muslih, the commander of Liwa al-Tafuf, the 13th brigade of the Popular Mobilization Forces (PMF) taking orders from the Jazira operations command, run by the U.S.-designated foreign terrorist organization, Kataib Hezbollah (KH).[21] These battle-hardened fighters would make their way back to Pakistan as the borders between Iran and Pakistan are open with the present political dispensation in Pakistan making sincere efforts for rapprochement with Iran.[22] The retribution of Hazaras and Shias would then be met with an equitable response from them and the civil strife in Pakistan would have another dimension which the Pakistan government would have no option but to use the heavy hand of military force which would further alienate the Shi'as in the Pakistan Army.[23] A Shi'a chat room running since early 1990s on the Internet has a trending argument that Shi'as in the Pakistan Army are attempting to hide their religious affiliations for fear of being ostracized and targeted.[24]

The US departure from Afghanistan and the return of the Taliban has opened a Pandora's Box of sectarian strife in the region with ripples reaching across the Durand Line. The attack on security forces in Chitral, the northern-most district of KPK, by the TTP was indicative of the TTPs propensity to expand its control over Shia-dominant areas to establish itself as champion of Deobandi/Salafi ideology.[25] The Shia-Sunni divide in the military is accentuated due to a creeping inflow of extreme Sunni religiosity wherein any one not aligned to the hard-line Salafi or Deobandi ideology needs to be culled.[26] General Bajwa faced a storm for his Ahmadiyya linkages in the national parliament when he took over as COAS in November 2016. In the recent past there have been stories alleging that General Asim Munir was a Shia.[27] The aim was to undermine the army chiefs; and indicative of the wedge in the military.[28] Religion has driven a chasm in the Pakistan military so deep that it may be called two militaries:[29] one of the state and the other of Islam with both charting trajectories for a collision.

Sectarianism (Intra Sect)

Recent headlines have warned that the 'intra-sectarian divide' in Pakistan is widening and intensifying[30] with violence in KPK, FATA and Baluchistan drawing sectarian fault lines within tribes.[31] The attack on a Barelvi procession in Mastung[32] on Eid Milad un-Nabi is a glaring example of violence precipitated to drive a chasm between Barelvi and Deobandi sects. The TLP and its leader, Saad Rizvi, have created a new realm of sectarian violence amongst Sunnis and with other sects of Islam holding the government hostage on blasphemy laws.[33] The domination of theological space in Pakistan and its affiliated clout in the state machinery has brought to the fore the dissonance between Deoband and Barelvi sects. Initial dissonance between Barelvi and Deobandi sects was over the sects' relative stance on the attributes of the Prophet Muhammad that have most widened the divide.[34] The ritual of the Barelvis compounded this doctrinal difference, particularly as they celebrated the birth of the Prophet. Milad-un-Nabi is characterized by processions in the streets, massive gatherings, celebrations and feasting. India and Pakistan have declared the day as a public holiday. This singular difference recently has led to deadly clashes between Deobandi and Barelvi groups on this date of the Islamic calendar. Some of the known attacks are listed below.

S. No.	Location	Date
01	DI Khan (KPK)	21 Nov 09
02	Jhang (Punjab)	11 Feb 12
03	Karachi (Sindh)	22 Jan 13
04	Islamabad (Capital Territory)	Dec 14
05	Kabul (Afghanistan)	30 Nov 17
06	Quetta (Baluchistan)	09 Nov 19
07	Mastung (KPK)	29 Sep 23

Fig. 9: Attacks on Milad-un-Nabi[35]

The TLP, a new entrant in a crowded eco-system of religious radicalism, is changing this and forcing everyone to pay attention. In a short span of less than a decade since its birth, it has forced two elected governments in Pakistan to accept the legitimacy of its ideology, pushed mainstream political parties to adopt some of its slogans, and created foreign policy challenges for a nuclear-armed nation that is seeking to make a geo-economic pivot to attract foreign investment, expertise, and trade. The Shia-Sunni divide has precipitated a situation where there is a race to occupy the top spot amongst Sunni organizations in their anti-Shia diatribe. Deobandis and Barelvi groups are facing off with each other in order to gain more credence as champions of Islam in Pakistan.[36] This face-off has created a chasm within the various sects of Sunni Islam and precipitated violence within them as well. There is another reason for the meteoric rise of Barelvi fundamentalism and that is the Pakistan Army and its fear of losing control over the theological space in Pakistan. The control of the terrorist groups in Pakistan which are Deobandi/Salafi in ideology slowly slipped out of the hands of the Deep State as the money flow to these groups was controlled by individuals and/or groups in West Asia and the Gulf countries. In order to develop a counter-narrative, Barelvi clerics were given a free hand. The army's support for the TLP is a coldly strategic calculation in order to undermine the TTP and its sympathizers among the so-called 'religious majority.' It also shows the army's simultaneous deployment of and vulnerability to religious languages of legitimacy. Even as officers themselves are becoming particularly Islamist, the army has always fused Islam and nation in ways that provide advantages in domestic politics but also make it difficult to credibly criticize and crack down on large swathes of Pakistan's Islamist landscapes, since they often use similar discourses and symbols.[37] The military perceives the TLP as a 'containable outfit' that can do its dirty work rather than making them hostile against the state.[38] Aligning with the army also helps the TLP to widen its base. Since the fall of Afghanistan to the Taliban, radical groups in Pakistan have become emboldened and question the democratic system in the country. The pro-army stance of the TLP is also evident from the fact that the assassination attempt on Imran Khan during a rally in November 2022 was by a TLP activist.[39] The military's patronage and an emotive religious issue of blasphemy have made the TLP an influential actor in Pakistan's politics. The civilian government's abject surrender to the TLP has set a dangerous precedent as future civilian governments too will be vulnerable to the coercive actions of extremist groups. The Taliban takeover of Afghanistan and an increasing tilt towards the 'centre-right' politics in Pakistan is only expected to strengthen groups like the TLP.

Barelvis enjoy a majority status in Pakistani demographics but have been identified with a more tolerant strain of Islam; the alignment to Sufi culture and religious tolerance had excluded them from the landscape of terror and violence. The mantle of terrorism and violence had squarely rested on the Deobandi sect till 2015 (Fig. 10).[40] The birth of the Deobandi and Barelvi sects is linked to the First War of Independence against the British in 1857 and the exile of Mughal King Bahadur Shah Zafar to Burma (Myanmar). The Crown ended the Mughal control of the subcontinent and also ended the primacy of Islam as the religion of the state. The clerics who so far had found a place in the elite were now part of the common people and in order to ensure the protection of Islam a movement was launched with a deep sense

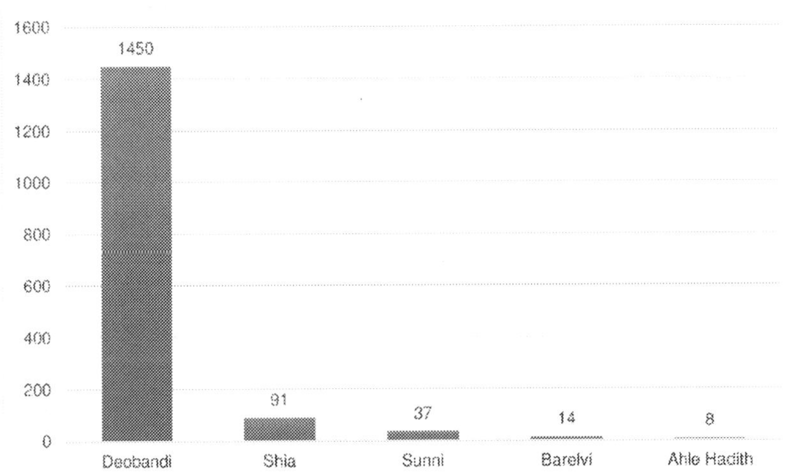

Fig. 10: Sectarian Affiliation of Terrorists Arrested in Pakistan, 2005-2011

of victimhood and a defining motivation to 'protect' Islam against hostile forces. Despite this, they are associated with devotion to Sufi saints and rituals being syncretic and not slave to strict written jurisprudence.

Deobandis too are Hanafi Sunni Muslims like the Barelvis, but they are more aligned and resemble the local variant of the extremist Salafi Islam born in Saudi Arabia. General Zia empowered their mullahs, mosques and madrassas during his regime; he thought it would protect his rule with endorsement by political entities like the JUI and also obtain external support from the House of Saud. The support to the Afghan Mujahideen was also predicated on his tom-tomming their cause which was aligned to the Deobandi sect. The Deobandis' influence, reach and relevance in a vast and volatile region like South Asia is immense. However, in September 2023, a Gallup survey in Pakistan revealed that the Saad Rizvi was Pakistan's second most popular leader after Imran Khan.[41] Deobandi presence in the KPK due to ideological alliances has metamorphosed into support for Imran Khan and his party, PTI, which has adopted a totally anti-armed forces stance[42] and thus is a pariah at the present. According to Shuja Nawaz in his book. *Crossed Swords: Pak, Its Army, and the Wars Within,"* politicians always invited the military to settle political differences amongst themselves. He wrote, "*Internally weak political parties tied to individual personalities or brought together by temporary and short-sighted common interests have turned to involve the army in political affairs, only to later lament its active role and taking over of the reins of power.*" The Deobandis and Salafis ultimately have contempt for national identities[43] and borders. The Tehreek-e-Jihad Pakistan, a new terrorist group operating along the Durand Line, has committed itself to the concept of *'Tehreek-e-Reshami Rumal'*, transcending national borders for formation of a trans-Asiatic *ummah*.

Ethnicity

The Punjabi-Pashtun détente was the reason for control over the Pakistan military and society. Historically, the bulk of the military was drawn from Punjab (about 71-75%), Pashtun (15-21%), Muhajir and Sindhis (3-5%) and Baloch (about 0.3%).[44] Thus, whether it was the armed forces or the bureaucracy, the Punjabi-Pashtun partnership held sway over ethnic groups like the Baloch and the Sindhis. The census of 2017 places the Punjabis at the top of the food chain both in terms of numbers and the heft they wield within the nation, while the Sindhis and Pashtuns are the other two ethnicities which are at 14.1 per cent and 15.4 per cent, respectively.[45] This eclectic ethnic tapestry has led to contestations and rivalry between these groups, adding to the complexity of Pakistan's demographic landscape. The nexus has ensured that the societal construct remains stable and aligned with the needs of the Punjabi elite. The same analogy also applies to the armed forces of Pakistan. Despite the attempt to recalibrate the class composition, the Pakistan military is still in the grip of the Punjab-Pashtun cohort.

Ser No.	Class	Previous % 2001	Current % 2007	Revised % 2011
01	Punjabi	71.06*	57.39	54.50
02	Pathan	13.65	14.18	14.50
03	Sindhi	15.00	15.40	17.00
04	Baluch	-	3.20	4.00
05	PoK & Northern Areas	-	9.11	9.00#
05	Minorities	0.29	0.72	1.00

* : Including PoK and Northern Areas 9.29%
# : Including PoK 7% & Northern Areas 2%

Fig. 11: Ethnic Composition of Pakistan Army[46]

Since the APS Peshawar attack, the high-handed punitive actions the military meted out to the entire KPK province as well as FATA has driven a wedge which has further been exacerbated by the deportation of the Afghan populace from

Pakistan.[47] Pakistan, on 3 October 2023 ordered all illegal immigrants, including 1.73 million Afghan nationals, to leave the country or face expulsion since 14 of 24 suicide bombings in Pakistan in 2023 were executed by Afghans.[48] The PTM has been fuelling a fire of ethno-nationalism amongst the Pashtuns[49] while large-scale internal displacement of the Pashtun population within Pakistan from KPK to Punjab and Sindh has created a Diaspora outside KPK which is willing to vector violence in other provinces of Pakistan as a response to any military action in KPK and/or FATA.[50]

At the same time, a growing alignment of citizenry in KPK and Baluchistan has begun to happen; the PTM supporting the BYC, led by Mahrang Baloch is a case in point.[51] On 2 January 2024, PTM had offered full support to the Baloch protest march[52] that had begun after a Baloch youth was allegedly killed in custody by the CTD in December 2023. Like the Pashtun Long March in 2019, both are part of a movement against the decade-long enforced disappearances and murder of innocent citizens. Solidarity between ethnic groups could and should be a sign of hope and a source of strength for all of them but also a matter of concern as the Punjabi majority witnessed the growth of a coalition against them. Baloch will find it easy to align with the Pashtuns for the return of the IDPs, end of collective punishments, end to the imperiousness of the security forces and a stop to the deportation of Pashtuns. Pashtuns will support the Baloch in their quest for resources and coast (i.e., the Gwadar sea port) and for safety of local interests in the CPEC. In the past, the PTM was not considered anti-state[53] and its struggle was for constitutionalism and fundamental rights, while, in contrast, the Baloch struggle was castigated as being foreign-funded secessionism, but now the same fate has befallen the PTM. The cohesion of Pashtun and Baloch movements will affect the cohesion of the Pakistan military.

The ethnic dissonance between various separatist groups in Pakistan prevented a co-option of their effort in the past as their ideologies and end states varied; however, in the recent past, a trend can be established wherein indications of broad-based coordination between Sindhi and Baloch groups with the TTP can be seen, both in intelligence-sharing as well as in adoption of doctrinal templates.[54] The employment of fedayeen attacks on Pakistan military strongholds by Baluch as in Mach[55] is a clear spin-off of the TTP's modus operandi visible in the attack on the Miyanwali airfield.[56] The ethnic groups within the Pakistan Army cannot be quarantined from the effects of such ethnic strife and its ramifications on the societal construct.

Conclusion

Galvanized by religion and ethnic loyalties which promote sub-nationalism, young Pakistan has become progressively less amenable to logic. A survey in 2011 of 2,000 Pakistanis of 18-27 years of age revealed that 75 per cent identify themselves as Muslims and only second as Pakistanis. If the same metrics are applied to the Pakistan military, the narrative of the divide may be well proven. It is this societal stress that has forced the Pakistan military top brass to resort to development of a new narrative of the Pakistan state.[57]

NOTES

1 https://openthemagazine.com/lounge/books/yuval-noah-harari-humanitys-storyteller/ accessed on 03 Jan 24.
2 HoodbhoyPervez, Pakistan, Origins, Identity & Future, Abingdon, New York NY, Routledge, 2023, p. 1.
3 https://indianexpress.com/article/explained/who-was-allama-iqbal-and-what-was-his-role-in-the-creation-of-pakistan-6080521/ accessed on 04 May 24.
4 Theodemocracy is a political system proposed by Joseph Smith, according to him it was a system under which God and people held the power to rule in righteousness. God was to be the ultimate power and would give law to the people, who would be free to accept or reject, presumably based on republican principles.
5 Independent or original interpretation of problems not precisely covered by the Qur'an, Hadith (traditions concerning the Prophet's life and utterances), and *ijma*.

6 Siddiqui Kalin M, N, Religious Authority and the Promotion of Sectarian Tolerance in Pakistan. United States Institute of Peace https://www.usip.org/sites/default/files/SR354_Religious-Authority-and-the-Promotion-of-Sectarian-Tolerance-in-Pakistan.pdf accessed on 12 Sep 19.

7 Zahab M. Abou, "The regional dimension of sectarian conflicts in Pakistan", in Pakistan, Nationalism without a Nation, (ed.) C. Jaffrelot (London, 2002), p. 116.

8 Ibid, p. 97.

9 https://www.webology.org/data-cms/articles/20220712020110pmwebology%2018%20(6)%20-%20530.pdf accessed on 15 Jan 24.

10 Refugee Review Tribunal, Australia, https://www.refworld.org/pdfid/4b6fe2e30.pdf accessed on 12 Sep19.

11 MarashiIbrahim, Re-conceptualizing Sectarianism in the Middle East and Asia https://www.mei.edu/publications/reconceptualizing-sectarianism-middle-east-and-asia accessed on 14 Aug 19.

12 Center for International Security and Cooperation (CISAC), at Freeman Spogli Institute for International Studieshttps://web.stanford.edu/group/mappingmilitants/cgi-bin/groups/view/147?highlight=April+19 accessed on 17 Aug 19.

13 Hassan Abbas, Pakistan's Drift into Extremism: Allah, the Army, and America's War on Terror (New York: M.E. Sharpe, Inc., 2005), p. 205; Amir Mir, The True Face of Jehadis (Lahore: Mashal Books, 2004), p. 170.

14 Sharan Sunil, Pakistan: A Shia leads a Sunni Army, https://timesofindia.indiatimes.com/blogs/strategic-insights/pakistan-a-shia-leads-a-sunni-army/ accessed on 14 Apr 24.

15 SoharwardySyed B.,Wahabization-Salafization of Pakistan and Muslim Ummah,Fighting the Terrorists But Supporting Their Ideology. https://www.islamicsupremecouncil.com/wahabization-salafization-of-muslims/ accessed on 14 Apr 24.

16 Ibid. pl check

17 Abdolrasool Divsallar & Hamidreza Azizi. (2024) Towards a non-Western model of security assistance: How Iran assists militaries. *Mediterranean Politics* 29:4, pp. 550-572.

18 https://www.memri.org/reports/50000-pakistani-shiite-pilgrims-go-missing-iraq-concern-deepens-over-irans-continuing accessed on 01 May 25.

19 https://www.aljazeera.com/news/2016/6/12/isil-claims-deadly-blasts-near-sayeda-zeinab-shrine accessed on 21 Nov 21.

20 https://www.washingtoninstitute.org/policy-analysis/hundreds-iran-backed-fatemiyoun-and-zainabiyoun-terrorists-warehoused-iraqi accessed on 11 May 25.

21 https://www.washingtoninstitute.org/policy-analysis/hundreds-iran-backed-fatemiyoun-and-zainabiyoun-terrorists-warehoused-iraqi accessed on 01 May 25.

22 https://en.irna.ir/news/85719696/Pakistani-PM-says-new-border-trade-route-with-Iran-to-provide accessed on 01 May 25.

23 Abdul Basit Khan, Implications of Syria-returning Zainabiyoun militants on

Pakistan's internal security. https://www.arabnews.com/node/1801476/amp accessed on 10 Apr 21.

24 https://www.shiachat.com/forum/topic/17796-shias-in-pakistani-military/ accessed on 04 May 25.

25 https://www.rferl.org/a/pakistani-taliban-land-grab-insurgency-islamabad/32595679.html accessed on 12 Oct 23.

26 ParvezHoodbhoy, Pakistan Army: Divided it Stands, Economic & Political Weekly, Vol. XLVI, June 25-Jul 8, 2011, Vol. 46, No. 26/27, pp. 67-68.

27 https://thefridaytimes.com/02-Apr-2023/nadra-inquiry-reveals-conspiracy-to-prevent-asim-munir-from-becoming-army-chief accessed on 22 May 24.

28 Sinha Rajiv, Pakistan Army: The Unyielding Guardian, https://www.orfonline.org/expert-speak/pakistan-army-the-unyielding-guardian accessed on 13 Apr 24.

29 Hoodbhoy, Pakistan Army: Divided it Stands, p. 68.

30 https://www.dw.com/en/pakistan-deadly-bomb-blast-at-sufi-shrine-in-lahore/a-48646054 accessed on 21 Sep 19.

31 https://www.brecorder.com/news/40252524/violent-conflict-in-kurram accessed on 25 Jul 23.

32 https://www.nytimes.com/2023/09/29/world/asia/pakistan-bombing.html accessed on 13 Oct 23.

33 Pattanaik Smruti S, TehrikLabaik Pakistan and the Politics of the Religious Right, 04 May 21, MP-IDSA Issue Brief, https://www.idsa.in/system/files/issuebrief/ib-tehrik-labaik-pakistan-sspattanaik-040521.pdf accessed on 05 May 21.

34 Weismann, Itzchak. "Sufi Fundamentalism between India and the Middle East." Sufism and the "Modern" in Islam, Martin Van Bruinessen and Julia Day Howell, ed. (London: I. B. Taurus, 2007), p. 117.

35 The compilation of these attacks have been done by the author based on news reports in various newspapers of Pakistan and Al Jazeera.

36 Z Sewag, The Intra-Sunni Conflicts in Pakistan. In: Syed, J., Pio, E., Kamran, T., Zaidi, A. (eds) Faith-Based Violence and Deobandi Militancy in Pakistan. Palgrave Macmillan, London. 2016, pp. 314-334.

37 https://paulstaniland.com/2017/12/03/the-pakistan-army-and-khadim-hussain-rizvi/ accessed on 04 May 25.

38 https://www.thefridaytimes.com/roots-of-rage-how-barelvi-militancy-became-a-mass-political-force/ accessed on 04 May 25.

39 https://www.thequint.com/opinion/imran-khan-assassination-attempt-trying-to-make-sense-of-chaos-in-pakistan-isi-military-peshawar accessed on 04 May 25.

40 https://islamanddiversity.org/2020/05/03/who-are-the-takfiri/ accessed on 21 Sep 24.

41 https://thediplomat.com/2023/10/saad-hussain-rizvis-soaring-popularity-and-pakistans-elections/#:~:text=In%20September%2 C%20a%20Gallup%20 Pakistan,compared%20to%20Khan's%2060%20percent. Accessed on 23 Mar 24.

42 Wolf Siegfried O, Imran Khan, the Military, and the Future of Pakistan, SADF

Research Report 9. 18 July, 2023 DOI: 10.48251/SADF.ISSN.2406-5641.RR9 ISSN: 2406-5641. Pg 3.

43 Guhl Jakob & Milo Comerford, Understanding the Salafi Online Ecosystem: A Digital Snapshot, https://www.isdglobal.org/wp-content/uploads/2021/11/Snapshot-study.pdf.

44 Siddiqa Ayesha, Pakistan Military: Ethnic Balance in the Armed Forces and Problems of Federalism, Forum of Federations in collaboration with the Centre for Civic Education –Pakistan and with support from the Republic of Germany, p. 11.

45 https://moderndiplomacy.eu/2023/10/21/from-the-two-nation-theory-to-regional-autonomy-movements-pakistans-identity-crisis/ accessed on 03 Jan 24.

46 Information Brief by DG ISPR- 2007, https://www.dawn.com/news/266159/punjab-s-dominance-in-army-being-reduced-ispr accessed on 10 Apr 23.

47 https://www.hrw.org/news/2023/11/28/pakistan-widespread-abuses-force-afghans-leave accessed on 12 Jan 24.

48 https://www.reuters.com/world/asia-pacific/pakistan-orders-all-illegal-immigrants-leave-after-suicide-bombings-2023-10-03/ accessed on 03 Jan 24.

49 Col. Harsh Vardhan Singh, Pashtun Tahafuz Movement (PTM) : Achilles Heel of Pak Army, published on 26 Mar 21 https://www.claws.in/pashtun-tahafuz-movement-ptm-achilles-heel-of-pak-army/

50 Shamil Shams, Pashtun 'ethnic profiling' in Pakistan, 2017, https://www.dw.com/en/why-pakistan-associates-terrorism-with-pashtuns-and-afghans/a-38024338 accessed on 10 Dec 23.

51 https://www.newsintervention.com/pashtuns-join-baloch-movement-against-pak-armys-atrocities-on-baloch-pashtuns/ accessed on 23 Feb 24.

52 https://thebalochistanpost.net accessed on 12 Jan 24.

53 Eleazar Sarah and Sher Ali Khan, *Anatomy of a Political Moment, Reportage from Pakistan on how a civil-rights movement is challenging Pakistan's status quo. The article was nominated for True Story Award 2019.*https://www.himalmag.com/politics/pasteen-tahafuz-protection-movement-rally-manzoor-pashteen-pakistan-rights accessed on 12 Mar 24.

54 https://www.icwa.in/show_content.php?lang=1&level =3&ls_id=10077& lid =6427 accessed on 09 Apr 24.

55 https://www.aljazeera.com/news/2024/1/30/at-least-10-killed-in-overnight-attack-by-baloch-rebels-in-pakistan accessed on 09 Apr 24.

56 https://www.aljazeera.com/news/2023/11/4/pakistan-kills-three-militants-foiling-attack-on-airbase accessed on 09 Apr 24.

57 Rashid Maria. 2021. *Dying to Serve: Militarism, Affect, and the Politics of Sacrifice in the Pakistan Army*. Lahore: Folio Books (Pakistan Edition), p. 221.

Four

Effect of Terrorism on the Military's Strategic Culture

Introduction

The Pakistan military's tryst with non-state actors or asymmetric warfare is as old as its inception. The perceived injustice of Partition forced the Pakistan military to look elsewhere to bridge the conventional asymmetry India enjoyed on the battlefield. The induction of Lashkars in 1947-48 led by Pakistani officers,[1] the use of infiltration columns in 1965[2] and the ingress in 1999 in Kargil sector are indicative of their propensity to use non-state actors with impunity against their eastern adversary.[3] However, the same is true even on the western borders, post the Afghan incursion in Bajaur in 1960[4] wherein Pakistan, contrary to popular belief, started supporting the Islamic groups in Afghanistan much before the Soviet invasion in 1979 as part of state policy to defend its territorial integrity from the concept of '*Pashtunistan*.'[5]

The use of terrorism as a tool of state policy is second nature to Pakistan; it was abetted by the USA and China in their appeasement of Pakistan. The US intervention was based on the use of the Pakistan military against the Soviet Union during the Cold War in the 1950s, wherein Pakistani forces underwent intensive training at Fort Bragg for guerrilla warfare; the raising of the SSG was the fruition of US efforts in preparing an asymmetric force in Pakistan.[6] The effort intensified as the Soviet invasion in 1979 created fears of further expansion of the Soviet Union into Pakistan. Jimmy Carter was warned by his NSA. "*I warned the President that the Soviets would be in a position, if they came to dominate Afghanistan, to promote a separate Baluchistan, which would give them access to the Indian Ocean while dismembering Pakistan and Iran.*"[7] The Pakistan officer corps, during their professional military education exposures in China, were introduced to the concept of guerrilla warfare and the use of non-state actors for weakening the adversary.[8] 'Protracted War', as a terminology, theorizes a military strategy penned by Mao Zedong, in *On Protracted War* (1938),[9] emphasizing long-term struggle and attrition, drawing the enemy into favourable terrain, and gradually escalating from guerrilla warfare to mobile warfare. In contemporary strategic thinking, it refers to a period characterized by prolonged military conflicts that lack decisive resolution, potentially leading to a gradual erosion of resources and morale. The ongoing Russia-Ukraine war and the Israel-Hamas war have become protracted and open-ended and are an anti-thesis to the Indian concept of a swift decisive conflict. If the reigning strategy of Pakistan against India is of a 'thousand cuts' and a 'thousand years', which implies protracted war, it must be planned for accordingly.

Non-state actors, as long as they did Pakistan's bidding, were a strategic weapon which to them was a slow but sure, inexpensive and effective response to conventional warfare and in consonance with their strategy of '*Bleeding India with a Thousand Cuts.*'[10] However, the tables turned when the same groups turned on their minders and started to target the Pakistani state and the Pakistan military. The policy of appeasement of these groups led to a ceasefire with the TTP many times; the Shakai Accord (2004), Sararogha Accord (2005), Waziristan Accord (2006) and the Nizam-e-Adl Agreement (2009)[11] is holding in some parts of FATA that has resulted in strengthening of the TTP. The ceasefires in

2019, 2021 and 2022 that were brokered by the Afghan Taliban have ended up hurting the military's capability to operate against the terrorist groups along the Durand Line.

Doctrinal Evolution

On the operational front, the military was forced to commit forces against terrorist organizations once President Musharraf was coerced into supporting the GWOT.[12] The forces inextricably got involved in OP ENDURING FREEDOM precipitating counter-action by terrorist groups on Pakistan and its security entities. Pakistan since 2001 has launched a series of operations under various names along the Durand Line in various parts of FATA and KPK. The Pakistan military is now operating under the ambit of OP AZM-E-ISTEHKAAM (Resolve of durable stability) to secure Chinese investments including the security of Chinese nationals.[13] Figure 12 depicts the location of these operations and their date lines.

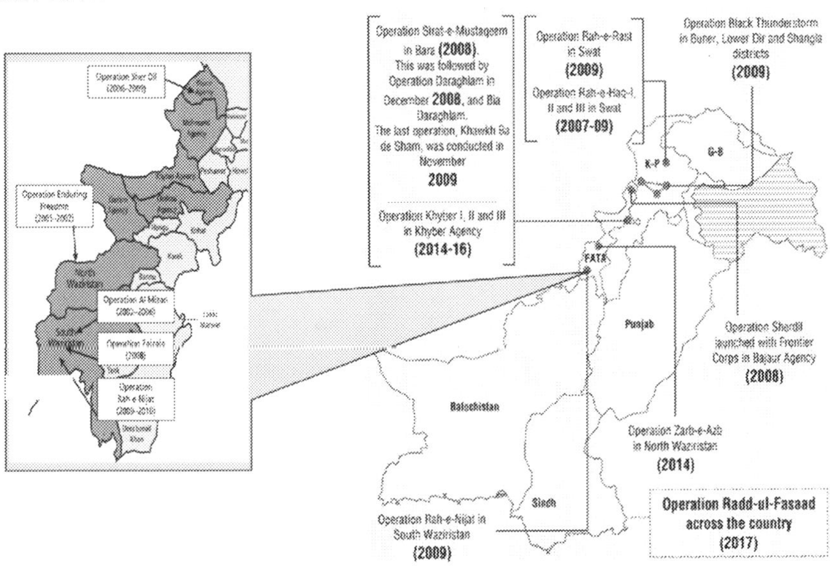

Fig. 12: Military Operations by Pakistan[14]

Counter-Insurgency Doctrine. The Pakistan military has used a heavy hand whenever employed within its own territory with little or no regard to collateral damage. Pakistan's National Assembly passed the anti-terror Pakistan Protection Bill in July 2014 to facilitate counter insurgency operations. The bill provided the Pakistani armed forces with extra-judicial powers to fight terrorism. It empowered Pakistani Army with powers; to arrest suspects and search houses without search warrants.[15] Several civil society and human rights organisations fears came true as these sweeping body-of-law further turned Pakistan into a hard police state. Pakistan's history is replete with examples where such laws have been abused. The strategy of punitive action adopted by the security forces in Baluchistan, FATA or even in Karachi has isolated the force from local support and antagonised the locals. The operational paradigm of '*Clear, Hold, Build and Transfer*'[16] inherited from the US forces entailed clearing an area of terrorist presence was always successful. However, the same did not hold true for the next three steps which demanded a population-centric approach. Once the forces withdrew, without resolving political, economic and societal challenges, the terrorists would return to assume control of governance and real estate. Under General Kayani, the Pakistan military finally adopted a counter-insurgency strategy.[17] Pakistan Army's counter insurgency strategy adopts a multipronged approach of kinetic operations clubbed with establishment and management of de-radicalisation centres in collaboration with the civilian government, urbanized policing, information operations, psychological operations, maintaining the Temporarily Displaced People (TDPs) and establishment of special courts. Similarly, military operation being conducted by Pakistan Army is to deny the geographical space clubbed with saturation of cognitive space with persuasion, dissuasion, coercion and punitive deterrence. The military training for the postmodern conflict demands different levels of preparation. It needs special training, battle expertise and career specialization. Pakistan Army's units undergo one year extensive pre-training for CI operations.[18] The

Directorate of Training and Evaluation in General Head Quarters (GHQ) critically evaluates this pre-training. Whereas officers who rotate out of CI operational environment are tasked to undertake 'train the trainee programmes'.[19] Moreover, Pakistan Military operates in home territory while recognizing cultural and social norms of various insurgent' areas as point of focus for training.

Converged Battle Domains (CBD). The positive effect of the operations in FATA and KPK has been the provision of a field lab for security forces to try out new concepts of war fighting with technology and multi-domain operations as the bulwark of future TTPs. The Pakistan military and law enforcement agencies have coordinated to achieve desired effects in OP ZARB-E-AZB. PAF, provided battle field situational awareness and real time ISR and precision strikes by both manned and un-manned platforms, regular forces and Frontier Corps-executed ground operations, while PN and Special Forces provided strategic results and communications, banking on cyber and space domains. Pakistani forces displayed coordination indicative of basic MDO that has been christened CBD.[20] The aim would be to coalesce tactical, operational and strategic operations from all domains to deliver the requisite effect. The objective of CBD would be to ensure deterrence and response options along the continuum of conflict against threats in all domains. Counter-insurgency training is now part of the PMA and School of Infantry and Tactics and is studied at Command and Staff College, Quetta, and the National Defence University. The Pakistan military now appears to be on an inexorable path towards developing and maintaining a counter-insurgency capability. While the military still retains its conventional force structure and stance vis-à-vis its arch rival, India, it appears to have used the insurgency to rotate its forces in and out of FATA and Swat in such a manner as to expose most of its regular troops to irregular warfare and also undergo live baptism by fire. The Frontier Corps (FC) has been trained by US trainers at Warsak in KPK. The military will benefit indirectly from this training and is supplementing it with overseas courses for its officers.

The Pakistan Army has increasingly embraced new-generation disruptive technologies to strengthen its counter-terrorism apparatus. Faced with persistent threats from both domestic and transnational terrorist groups, the army has recognized the need to evolve beyond conventional methods of warfare and surveillance. One of the most significant technological advancements in Pakistan's counter-terrorism strategy is the deployment of Unmanned Aerial Vehicles (UAVs). Indigenous drones such as Burraq and Shahpar have been developed for surveillance and precision strikes, particularly in the former Federally Administered Tribal Areas (FATA).[21] These drones offer real-time intelligence, surveillance, and reconnaissance (ISR), enabling the military to identify and eliminate high-value targets with greater accuracy and minimal collateral damage.[22] The indigenous development has been complemented by the acquisition of TB-2 and Akinci UCAV from Turkey and the Wing Loong series from China.[23] Complementing aerial surveillance is the enhanced use of Signals Intelligence (SIGINT) and Electronic Intelligence (ELINT). Intelligence agencies such as the Inter-Services Intelligence (ISI) and Military Intelligence (MI) have upgraded their capabilities to intercept militant communications, track mobile phones, and triangulate locations of suspects. These tools have been crucial in urban counter-terrorism operations as well as in targeting terrorist hideouts in remote areas.

Pakistan has also made strides in geospatial intelligence by the launch of its own remote sensing satellites, including PRSS-1 and PakTES-1A.[24] These satellites provide high-resolution imagery that aids in monitoring border infiltration routes, mapping difficult terrains, and identifying militant compounds. The strategic application of such satellite data has improved the military's situational awareness and response time during operations. Another critical domain in the fight against terrorism is cyber surveillance including the raising of a cyber command.[25] As extremist groups increasingly exploit the Internet for recruitment and propaganda, Pakistani agencies have developed the capacity to monitor social media platforms and shut down radical websites. The Federal Investigation Agency's (FIA) cyber crime wing, in coordination with the Pakistan Telecommunication Authority (PTA), plays a central role in this digital vigilance. These institutions work to detect and disrupt online terrorist networks and foil attempts at cyber-radicalization.[26] Moreover, data analytics and artificial intelligence (AI) are becoming integral to predictive counter-terrorism strategies. The Pakistan Army's Computerized Decision Support System (CIDSS) uses Big Data analytics to process vast amounts of intelligence from various sources, enabling commanders to anticipate patterns of militant behaviour and respond proactively. These AI-driven systems offer the military a strategic advantage by turning raw intelligence into actionable insights.

In urban centres, the integration of biometric and facial recognition technologies has strengthened law enforcement efforts. Pakistan's national database authority, NADRA,[27] maintains extensive biometric records, which are utilized in identifying suspects and verifying identities at checkpoints. This is further supported by safe city projects in cities like Lahore, Karachi, and Islamabad, where high-definition CCTV cameras with facial recognition capabilities help monitor public spaces and prevent terrorist attacks.[28] On the borders, particularly along the Pakistan-Afghanistan frontier, Pakistan has invested in smart border management systems. These include thermal imaging, motion sensors, and biometric verification systems installed at major crossings such as Torkham and Chaman.[29] These tools have proven effective in curbing the movement of militants and smuggling of arms, thus enhancing border security. The military and police have also begun using robotics and remote-controlled technologies for bomb disposal and surveillance in high-risk environments. These systems reduce the risk to personnel and improve the effectiveness of counter-IED (improvised explosive device) operations, particularly in urban warfare scenarios. Lastly, Integrated Command and Control Systems (ICCS) allow for real-time coordination between various arms of the military and law enforcement. These systems link field units, intelligence grids, and emergency response teams to streamline operations and reduce response time during terror incidents. Despite these advancements, challenges remain. Pakistan's reliance on foreign technology, particularly from China and Turkey, raises concerns about long-term sustainability and cyber security. Additionally, the lack of centralized coordination among intelligence agencies can create operational inefficiencies. There is also an ongoing debate about privacy concerns stemming from increased surveillance in civilian areas, highlighting the need for balanced oversight and legal safeguards. Pakistan's incorporation of new-generation technologies into its counter-terrorism strategy marks a significant shift towards more sophisticated and effective operations. While traditional methods remain essential, the integration of drones, cyber tools, AI, biometrics, and smart surveillance has empowered the country to respond to terrorism with greater precision and foresight. Continued investment in indigenous innovation, inter-agency collaboration, and ethical governance will be critical for sustaining these gains and ensuring a secure future.

Societal Evolution

The Pakistan military may have gained from conduct of CI operations along its western borders but there has been unintended negative fallout in the cognitive domain. The counter-response has been in the conduct of an annual event of *Youm-e-Takreem Shuhada-e-Pakistan* (Martyrs' memorial) at GHQ, Rawalpindi. This event has become an important public relations exercise for the military to counter the narrative of home-grown Islamist insurgency in KPK.[30] The fatwa issued by the Imam of Lal Masjid post Op SILENCE wherein he decreed that troops killed fighting jihadis would not be considered martyrs and would not be allowed burial in Islamic cemeteries created a societal crisis.[31] The famous poem by Wilfred Owen, *Pro Patria Mori*,[32] meaning 'to die for one's country' written during WW I and published in 1920 is now being used by the military in an ongoing shift in the narrative of sacrifice, from an overbearing pan-Islamic conception to a more territorial-centric comprehension of nationhood.

The slogan '*sab se pehle Pakistan*'[33] (Pakistan first) was a conscious effort on the part of the military to distance itself from the legacy of General Zia. There is a conscious effort by the military to replace the previous singular emphasis on religious martyrdom with the more composite territorial concept of dying for the homeland. Participation in GWOT led to religious parties and groups affiliated with sectarian outfits to contest the decision of joining the American war by calling it a betrayal of both Afghans and Islam. This relationship between religious militant groups like the TTP and the military has started to grow tense which has resulted in a spate of suicide attacks on military personnel and other LEAs. Military operations in Swat and the erstwhile FATA districts of KPK have forced the top army brass to review the policy on *jihad* and the use of religious vocabulary. Distinctions were made between *asal shaheed* (the real martyr) and those who died fighting religious militants in Swat and FATA. The real martyrs were those who died fighting on Indian borders, while the ambivalence about martyrs on the western borders comes from the fact that the enemy was itself Muslim.

Labours at coalescing religious ideals of martyrdom with the conception of '*dying for the homeland*' leads to tensions, both extraneous and intrinsic, and to the military. One key reason for this is the inability of the military to control the doctrinal interpretation of religion or to completely monopolize the use of the label of *shahadat*. The dependence of the military on the affective repertoire of Islam further complicates the goal of winning the counter-insurgency domain and ending ambiguities about the future course of action regarding state making and nation building.[34] The situation becomes even more complicated with the Taliban's victory in Afghanistan, as it will further erode the control of the military regarding the use of religious symbols and doctrines to meet its institutional ends.

Pakistan Military in Terrorist Outfits

The armed forces of Pakistan have historically played a pivotal role in the country's politics, national identity and security architecture. With a long-standing tradition of discipline, professionalism, and commitment to national defence, the Pakistan military is one of the most powerful institutions in the country. However, in recent decades, Pakistan has faced the complex challenges of religious extremism and terrorism, which have not only affected civilian society but has also penetrated segments of the security establishment. A particularly troubling phenomenon is the involvement of serving or retired military personnel in terrorist or extremist groups. To understand why some military personnel have joined or supported terrorist groups, it is essential to consider Pakistan's historical and strategic context. Since the 1980s, Pakistan's security agencies have had a complicated relationship with Islamist militant groups. During the Soviet Afghan War, the Inter-Services Intelligence (ISI) with US and Saudi support, trained and supported Afghan mujahideen. This period saw the normalization of jihadist ideology in parts of the security apparatus, creating long-term ideological spillovers.[35] Moreover since the 1990s, the Pakistani Deep State has supported Kashmiri militant groups like the Lashkar-e-Taiba (LeT) and the Jaish-e-Mohammed (JeM) to unleash terror against India. Most recently, Hashim Musa, one of two Pakistani terrorists identified by investigators in connection with the 22 April 2025 Pahalgam terror attack, is a former regular of the Pakistan Army's para forces. The Pakistan Army dismissed Musa from its ranks, after which he joined the banned terrorist group, LeT. It is believed he infiltrated into India in September 2023. A source in the security establishment is of the view that Musa may have been asked by the Pakistan Army's Special Service Group (SSG) to join the LeT and strengthen the terror outfit's Kashmir operations.[36] While these policies are driven by strategic calculations, they also blurred the line between national interest and ideological alignment, creating conditions where some military personnel became sympathetic to or were radicalized by extremist ideologies.[37]

While most of Pakistan's military personnel serve honourably, a small but significant number of cases involving terrorist links have come to light, especially in the past two decades. One of the most high-profile cases was that of Brigadier Ali Khan, a senior officer in the Pakistan Army who was arrested in 2011. He was charged with ties to the banned radical organization, the Hizb ut-Tahrir (HuT), which seeks to establish a global Islamic caliphate. According to military sources, Khan had long-standing Islamist leanings and reportedly criticized Pakistan's cooperation with the USA in the 'War on Terror'.[38] In September 2014, the Pakistan Navy foiled an audacious terrorist plot when militants attempted to hijack a naval frigate, the *PNS Zulfiqar*, at the Karachi dockyard. Investigations later revealed that the attackers included former naval officers. The attackers were allegedly linked to al-Qaeda in the Indian Subcontinent (AQIS). This plot exposed alarming vulnerabilities within the navy and showed that military training and insider knowledge could be exploited by terrorist networks.[39] A military court in 2019 had found a brigadier and a lt. general guilty of espionage, sentencing one to death and handing 14 years of 'rigorous imprisonment' to the other.[40] There have been persistent allegations that former ISI operatives and other military retirees maintain ties with groups like the Afghan Taliban and the Haqqani Network. While not all such links are criminal or direct, some involve ideological sympathies, informal support, or shared operational histories.[41] In 2008, Lieutenant General Mushtaq Baig, the Surgeon-General of the Pakistan Army, was killed in a suicide bombing in Rawalpindi. Although the attacker was not from the military, the assassination demonstrated the extent to which terrorists had penetrated high-security zones and were targeting senior military figures.[42]

Understanding why military personnel may turn to extremist groups requires examining both institutional and individual factors. Some individuals in the armed forces are drawn to extremist ideologies, especially those rooted in pan-Islamism or anti-Western narratives. The extensive exposure to Islamic teachings in the broader society, combined with disillusionment with Western foreign policy, can make some soldiers susceptible to religious extremism.[43] Personnel who believe that Pakistan is compromising Islamic values by aligning with Western powers can become ideologically alienated. For example, the post-9/11 alignment with the USA in the 'War on Terror' angered many Islamists, including some within the military, who saw it as a betrayal of Afghan jihadist allies.[44] The involvement of military personnel in terrorism has serious implications for Pakistan's internal stability and international standing. When insiders leak sensitive information or use their training for terrorist purposes, the threat to critical infrastructure multiplies. Such breaches undermine trust in the armed forces and compromise operations. Pakistan already faces international scrutiny over its alleged links with terrorist groups. Cases involving military personnel deepen concerns among global partners, affecting military aid, foreign investment and diplomatic relations. These incidents point to the need for greater civilian oversight of the military and intelligence services. However, the Pakistan military has historically resisted civilian accountability, and efforts to investigate military conduct, especially regarding extremism, are often blocked or deflected.

The phenomenon of military personnel joining or aiding terrorist groups in Pakistan is a serious threat hovering on margins of becoming unmanageable. While only a small minority of individuals are involved, their actions have outsized consequences. These cases reveal vulnerabilities in institutional ideology, accountability and recruitment practices. Jinnah's dream for the 'land of the pure' has been sacrificed to the two beasts of violent religious extremism and militarism. "*Depending on who you asked, Islam or the army were supposed to be the glue holding the place together, yet both, in their own way, seemed to be tearing it apart.*"[45] Declan Welsh in his book, *The Nine Lives of Pakistan* makes this very incisive remark which defines the Pakistan military today. If Islam was not enough, politics has now made inroads into the Pakistan Army with fissures appearing on the ground of support to deposed Prime Minister Imran Khan and his party, the PTI, while the loyalists to the military establishment have taken a tough line against the cricketer-turned–politician; but there is a sizeable fan following within the armed forces which is rooting for his return to power. Imran is believed to still enjoy support in the army and army families. Many might not be openly supporting Imran because it can create problems for them, but the support exists.[46] The sacking of high ranking army officers after the 9 May 2023 riots was an indication of the support accorded by some of the officers incarcerated for not taking action against the rioters as their sympathies lay with the arrested leader.[47] Pakistan's military has charged Lieutenant General Faiz Hamid, the former head of Pakistan's Inter-Services Intelligence (ISI), with 'engaging in political activities', in essence accusing him of working with ex-Prime Minister Imran Khan to destabilise the nation.[48] The support to the deposed leader has not waned and the supporters have directed their ire against the COAS, Gen. Asim Munir, which was very evident in an open letter written to the General by a group of Pakistan Army personnel, including colonels, majors, captains and soldiers, calling for General Asim Munir to resign immediately. They accused him of misusing military power to suppress political opposition, silence journalists and undermine democratic processes.[49] So far, the army had fractured the political landscape of the country but for the very first time it seems that it is getting a dose of its own medicine as it sees a chasm opening up between various factions based on political affiliations.

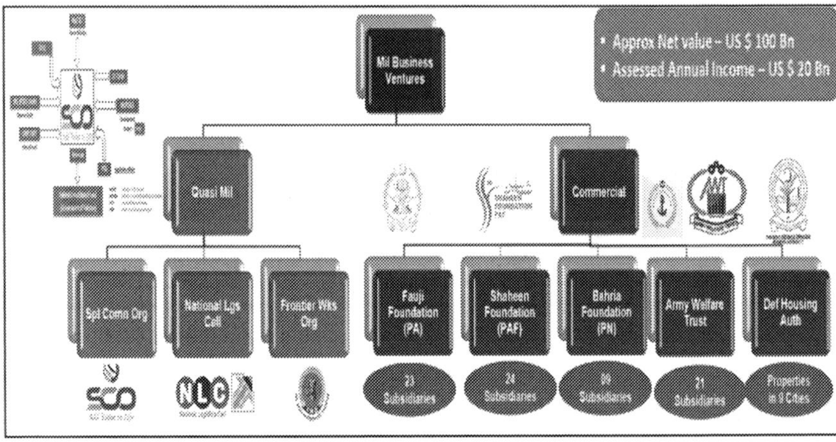

Fig. 13: MILBUS Organogram in Pakistan

Pakistan's Military Business (MILBUS)

The proliferation of terrorist actions brought to the fore the vulnerability of the Pakistan military's core asset of MILBUS. The term 'MILBUS' was coined by Ayesha Siddiqia in her book, *Military Inc—Inside Pakistan's Military Economy,* and refers to the involvement of the military in economic activities beyond their purview. MILBUS has been defined as "*Military capital used for personal benefit of military fraternity, especially the officer cadre, which is not recorded as part of defence budget or does not follow the normal accountability procedures of the state, making it an independent genre of capital. It is either controlled by the military or under its implicit or explicit patronage.*" The more widespread the shroud of terrorism spreads, the more damaging is the loss to MILBUS. The primacy of MILBUS in the Pakistan military's strategic culture is a new insertion into the calculus and does affect their behavioural pattern.

The Pakistan military's foray into the economy commenced in 1954, when the first welfare organization, *Fauji Foundation,* was established.[50] It received its initial corpus from the British as part of Pakistan's share of the Post War Service Reconstruction

Fund, established in 1942 for veterans of WW II. Siddiqa details how the military economy of Pakistan revolves around four welfare foundations which are run by the individual services.[51] What distinguishes the Pak military business complex is its level of independence and autonomy from any form of overarching control. The Fauji Foundation (General Staff), Army Welfare Trust (Army), Shaheen Foundation (Air Force) and the Bahria Foundation (Navy), are run by their respective services, and the Ministry of Defence has no control over their business operations. Pakistan is on the verge of an economic meltdown, weighed down by harsh payback terms from international lenders. With only $ 5.2 billion worth of state reserves and a debt of over $ 13.5 billion owed to the International Monetary Fund, the army nonetheless received an increased payment of $ 11.27 billion in last year's budget. Between 2011 and 2015 alone, the army's assets grew by 78 per cent.[52] By 2016, the armed forces in Pakistan ran over 50 commercial entities, including public sector organisations and real estate ventures worth $ 30 billion. Today, their commercial assets are worth over $ 39.8 billion. Top military officers, including former army chief, General Qamar Jawed Bajwa, and army spokesman, General Asim Saleem Bajwa, have been revealed to have experienced significant financial gains within a relatively short time. Bajwa's immediate family amassed substantial wealth, becoming billionaires within six years. General Asim Saleem Bajwa and his brother established a business empire that included 133 restaurants across four countries, operating under the Papa John's pizza franchise.[53] An investigation was also launched into real estate corruption by the brothers of former army chief, Ashfaq Parvez Kayani, who, for many years was the most powerful figure in the country. The Pandora Papers exposed a long list of Pakistan's former military officers who had accumulated immense wealth through tax evasion and corruption. Over time, the military's economic interests have gained prominence. This includes military-owned businesses, significant onshore and offshore land and property holdings and influence over defence contracts.

In 2016, in a written reply to a question asked in parliament, Defence Minister Khwaja Asif informed the house that there were nearly 50 "projects, units and housing colonies" functioning in the country under the administrative control of the foundations.[54] A company under the name of Pak Maroc Phosphor SA was set up in Morocco by the Fauji Foundation in 2008 for international intervention as well. Profits from these enterprises are used to fund the respective services directly and remain opaque. Siddiqa estimates that between 2004 and 2006, the Fauji Foundation received an estimated USD 65 mn in subsidies, a sum which no private sector business group has ever received.[55] The magnitude is visible from the turnover of the Fauji Foundation in 2021 (Fig. 14).

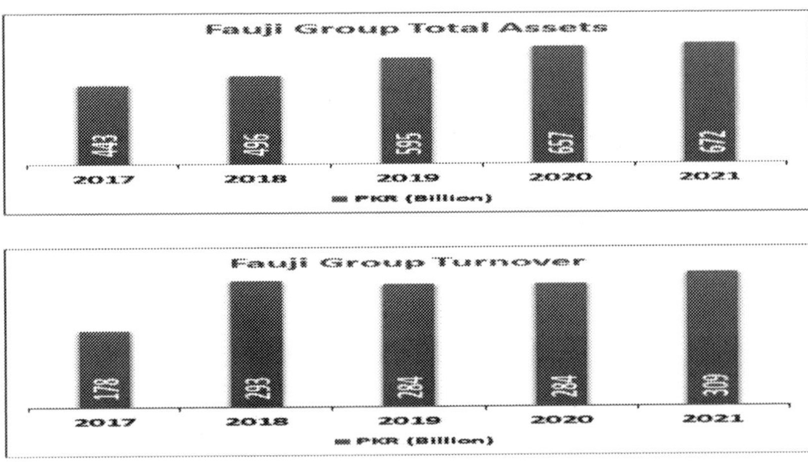

Fig. 14: Financial Overlay of Fauji Foundation[56]

The military's economic activities have morphed into a hybrid structure that integrates with private business enterprises (often illegal) as a means of supplementing personal income and amassing wealth. Rather, the military's participation in the economy creates major vulnerabilities which compromise the degree of professionalism of the military and also governs their behavioural patterns and response to criminal gangs with terrornarco nexus. The slowdown of the Pakistani economy was bound to have a direct effect on the MILBUS which forced a response from GHQ to ensure that the economic ecosystem of the country was stabilised to ensure an uninterrupted flow of funds from the MILBUS into the military organization.

Part of Chinese President Xi Jinping's flagship Belt and Road Initiative, the aim of a $ 64-billion project, is to shorten oil, gas, and other trade routes by thousands of kilometres by cutting overland from western China rather than going around South and Southeast Asia by ship. The CPEC is not an arrangement between two governments but an understanding reached between the Pakistan Army, the Chinese government and private agencies. The stakes of the Pakistan Army in the project are vital to its fruition and a key to maintenance of the Pakistan Army's MILBUS. The CPEC Authority Bill passed in 2020 allows the chairman of the CPEC Authority absolute control over the project.[57] As per the official website of the Pakistan Army, the Frontier Works Organization, the army's construction, and engineering arm, "has constructed 3,797 km of roads" in the past 30 years, "besides preparing eight completely new airfields and upgrading 11 others."[58] Since the FWO has contracts for building roads as part of the CPEC, the army would benefit from any mining that will happen under CPEC. However, with Baluch separatists targeting the CPEC projects and, in the recent past, even the TTP turning its attention to CPEC projects to cause pain to the Pakistan Army, has caused it to commit forces for the security of the projects. In the last four years, 62 people working on the China-Pakistan Economic Corridor (CPEC) have been killed in eight attacks across Pakistan;[59] two attacks on Chinese engineers working on CPEC projects took place in Baluchistan, four in Sindh and two in Khyber Pakhtunkhwa. Notably, the Baloch Liberation Army (BLA) Majeed Brigade has been behind most of the high-profile attacks on Chinese citizens working on the CPEC project.

While China has publicly affirmed its confidence in Pakistan's capacity to handle security threats to bilateral infrastructure projects, there are growing signs of Chinese impatience. The GHQ at Rawalpindi is pursuing military responses in tandem with economic development as a long-term answer to its security problems. The raising of two light infantry divisions funded by the Chinese for security has not yielded the desired results.[60] Countering terrorism has become a renewed priority for Pakistan, amid growing Chinese impatience at persistent insecurity along the CPEC. This economic development project which includes coal-fired power plants, highways and fresh-water facilities has been the subject of much scrutiny over its progress. Given Pakistan's current economic challenges and the importance of Chinese investments, Islamabad is taking significant measures to counter terrorist activity that may target the CPEC. Its strategy is twofold: it is committing a large number of conventional forces to expedite the counter terrorist operations under OP AZM-E-ISTEKAM[61] and also opening avenues for private security companies to take over security duties at some of the key projects.

In normal course, Pakistan's laws prohibit foreign Private Military Companies (PMCs) and Private Security Companies (PSCs) to work independently in the country. In addition, the local PSCs in Pakistan are highly regulated in terms of licences to carry arms and their operations. Yet, Pakistani laws do not prohibit foreign PSCs to enter into joint ventures with local PSCs. This is a significant avenue for Chinese PSCs to work around local laws to expand their activities.[62] Most Chinese PSCs work through this legal loophole in Pakistan. At present, it is appreciated that 15 PSCs are operating within Pakistan. They are listed in Figure 15.

S. No.	Name of Company	Major Area of Operation	Remarks	Year
1.	Beijing Dewei Security Co. Ltd.	Pakistan; BRI focus.	Entirely staffed by PLA veterans and retired PSB personnel.	2011
2.	China Security and Protection Group Co. Ltd.	Southeast Asia and South Asia focus; presence in Sri Lanka and Myanmar.	Works with major Chinese companies in Pakistan; it has two branches: China Security Technology Group Pakistan established in 2016 and China Security Technology Group Pakistan in 2017 (only foreign PSC to establish local branch without collaboration).	1994
3.	Huaxin Zhong'an Security Co. Ltd.	Maritime domain; works with a Pakistan PSC linked to Pakistan Navy.	Maritime escort; risk assessment; anti-piracy in Western Indian Ocean.	2004
4.	Shanghai Zhong Chengwei Security Service Group Co. Ltd.	Pakistan, South Africa, Columbia, Brazil, Dubai.	Armed escort, risk assessment and consultancy for large Chinese construction companies.	2005
5.	Shenzhen Zhongzhou Special Security Consultant Co. Ltd.	Focus on BRI in Asia; no reported presence in Pakistan so far.	—	2006
6.	China Overseas Security Group (consortium of 5 Chinese PSCs)	Pakistan; major focus on BRI.	—	2015
7.	Frontier Services Group (FSG)	Myanmar and Pakistan in South Asia; major BRI focus.	Established by Eric Prince, former Backwater boss, it has established two forward bases in Yunnan and Xinjiang; expertise in training, risk assessment and intelligence collection.	2014
8.	Shandong Huawei Security Group	Pakistan	First Chinese security company to establish overseas branch in 2010.	1993
9.	Beijing Dingtai Anyuan Security Co. Ltd.	Pakistan, Afghanistan, Iraq.	—	2011
10.	Beijing Guang'an Security and Tech Co. Ltd.	Afghanistan and Pakistan.	—	2008
11.	Genghis Security Academy	No reported presence in Pakistan.	Training bodyguards for Chinese PSCs.	2011

S. No.	Name of Company	Major Area of Operation	Remarks	Year
12.	Beijing Dujie Security Technology Co. Ltd. (part ofthe China Overseas Security Group)	Local branchin Pakistan, the Pan-Asia Group.	Risk assessment, security awareness and trainingfor Chinese nationals, including live fire drills and consultancy.	2011
13.	Zhongjie Security Group	BRI focus.	Reports on its website about an MoU with local PSC in Pakistan.	2016
14.	.Weizhijie Security Ltd.	Pakistan	Recruits PLA veterans; focus on Karachi and Baluchistan.	2002
15.	Huai'an Security Limited	Pakistan and Vietnam	—	1988

Fig. 15: List of Chinese PSCs Operational in Pakistan[63]

Chinese PSCs face several challenges while operating in Pakistan the issue of cultural understanding and the lack of trained staff proficient in Urdu or other local languages gets pronounced in rural areas where tribal norms and ethics run the course of life. The via media has been found by creating an arrangement of convenience with Pakistani PSCs. Pakistan has many PSCs, for instance, Askari Guards[64] is a security company with links with Chinese PSCs. It has been involved closely with the Pakistani military and has a strong presence in the restive regions of Federally Administered Tribal Areas (FATA), Baluchistan and Khyber Pakhtunkhwa.[65] For the Chinese PSCs, working with local PSCs in Pakistan provides a convenient mechanism to function in the country. The overwhelming dominance of the Pakistan military with the Adjutant-General of the Pakistan Army as chairman on the board of directors of the Askari Guards, which is a subset of Askari Foundation points to the military taking a sure but circuitous route for benefiting from the Chinese presence. Chinese PSCs work with local PSCs to circumvent local laws and maintain a low profile, thereby avoiding the limelight. Indeed, Chinese PSCs in Pakistan have done this successfully and, despite official denial, their presence has increased manifold, with unofficial linkages with the Pakistan Army and navy, other state agencies and local PSCs. In addition, the PSCs work for both government and private enterprises in Pakistan. The Chinese PSCs have become a convenient tool to influence operations and shaping the cognitive domain of the military establishment, the use of non-military and non-diplomatic means to extend China's influence in other countries. With China willing to spend on influencing operations using a variety of means and tools, particularly in its immediate neighbourhood in Asia,[66] such a possibility involving PSCs cannot be ruled out in the future; although their role in this regard remains unclear so far.

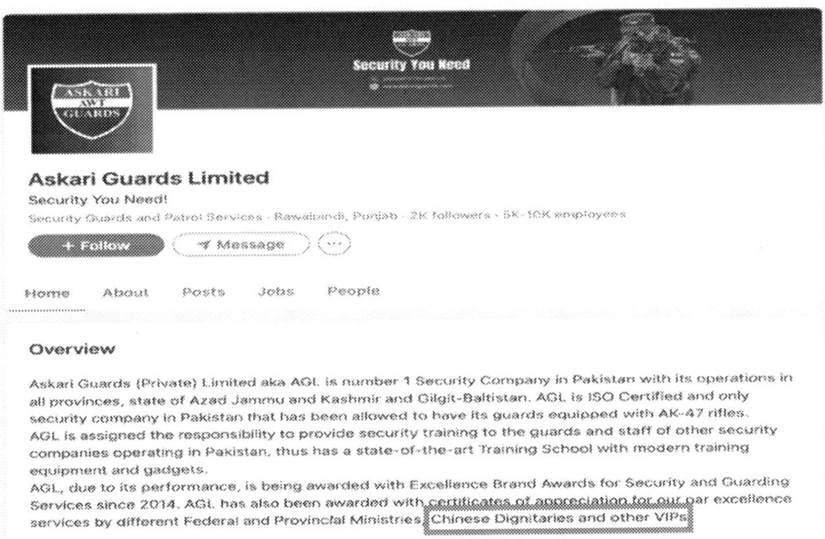

Fig. 16: LinkedIn Page of Askari Guards

Two Chinese companies, the Beijing Dewei Security Co. Ltd., and Weizhijie Security Co. Ltd., perform the tasks of security assessment, analysis, consultancy, and awareness, as also indirect security tasks by working with the Askari Guards. Furthermore, at the behest of Chinese policymakers, the PSCs may become a crucial mechanism for cultivating local groups within the military, so as to influence the decision making over a period of time. This will have serious implications for other countries trying to deal with China's presence and influence in their foreign, security and economic policies. While China has engaged with the Pakistan military establishment heavily, it has hesitated to cultivate local extremist groups due to its sensitivity over potential spill over in Xinjiang. Still, such a possibility cannot be denied as the country attempts to manage the security of its assets overseas with respect to non-extremist groups. China is known to have deep pragmatic connections with rebels and militants in countries like Myanmar,[67] which provides a perspective on whether and how it engages with non-state actors in countries with political instability. Such involvement will also add to the intense strategic competition with the USA and other powers, including India.

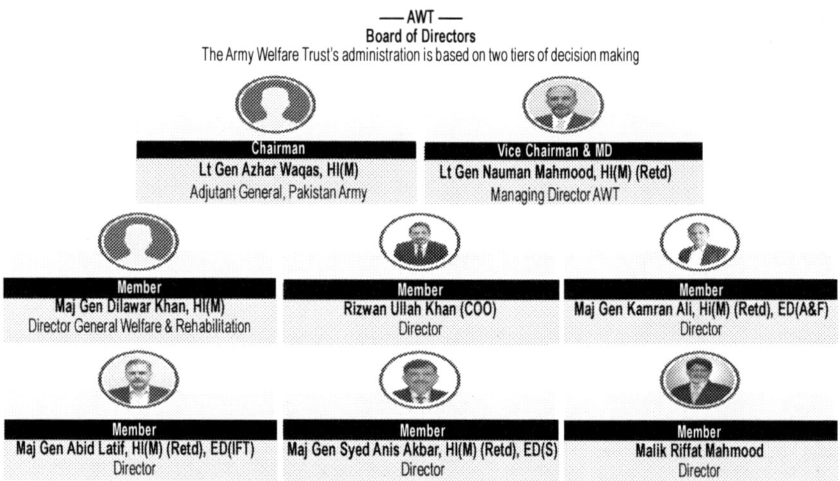

Fig. 17: Board of Directors: Askari Guards[68]

Conclusion

Terrorism has led to structural and organizational infirmities in the Pakistan military. These infirmities impact human resource management wherein the recruitment patterns, motivation to serve and idea of martyrdom have been re-calibrated. More importantly, for the elite within the Pakistan Military, it has dented their business conglomerate which is under duress due to the economic doldrums Pakistan is in. The security situation has become so exacerbated that foreign investment is hard to come by despite the aggressive actions of SIFC; even the all-weather ally, China, has expressed its deep concern over the safety of Chinese assets and personnel in Pakistan.[69] The recent attacks on Chinese workers[70] is one of the triggers for OP AZM-E-ESTAKAM to be launched by the Pakistan armed forces[71] which, as per the Defence Minister of Pakistan, may even entail cross-border strikes in Afghanistan[72] creating conditions for a violent response by the Taliban or its proxies in Pakistan. The linkages of terrorism with Pashtun sub-nationalism and the political enterprise of Imran Khan have created a public perception against the Pakistan military which has dented its standing in the nation.

NOTES

1 Tamiri Ramesh, Pakistan Invasion on J&K (1947–48) Untold Stories of Victims,Oberoi Book Service, Jammu (2024), p. 23.

2 Ganguly Sumit, The Crisis in Kashmir: Portents of War, Hopes of Peace, Cambridge, U.K.: Cambridge University Press, 1999.

3 Tellis Ashley J., C. Christine Fair, and Jamison Jo Medby, Limited Conflicts Under the Nuclear Umbrella: Indian and Pakistani Lessons from the Kargil Crisis, MG-1450-USCA, Santa Monica, Calif.: RAND Corporation, 2001.

4 Keesings Record of World Events,Volume-07, Jun 1961, p. 18172, https://web.stanford.edu/group/tomzgroup/pmwiki/uploads/1303-1961-06-KS-AJG.pdf accessed on 18 Apr 24.

5 Ibid, p. 18173.

6 Nawaz Shuja, Crossed Swords: Pakistan, Its Armyand the Wars Within, New York, Oxford University Press, 2008, p. 45.

7 Brzezinski Zbigniew, Power and Principle: Memoirs of the National Security Adviser, 1977–1981, New York: Farrar, Straus, and Giroux, 1983, p. 427.

8 Cohen Stephen, *The Idea of Pakistan, Washington, D.C.: Brookings, 2004*, p. 105. Cohen cites Shafi, "The Effectiveness of Guerrilla War," p. 11.

9 https://www.marxists.org/reference/archive/mao/selected-works/volume-2/mswv2_09.htm accessed on 03 May 25.

10 https://www.mea.gov.in/articles-in-indian-media.htm?dtl/15916/Buying+peace+for+bombarded+borders accessed on 10 May 24.

11 Accord was signed between ANP government in Khyber-Pakhtunkhwa and the outlawed Tehreek-e-Nifaz-e-Shariat-e-Muhammadi (TNSM). Nizam-e-Adl established a parallel judicial system in the country based on Sharia law.

12 Dr Yamin Tughral, Examining Pakistan's Strategic Decision to Support the US War on Terror, Centre for International Peace & Stability, NUST Islamabad, p. 114. https://issi.org.pk/wp-content/uploads/2016/05/Tughral-Yamin-35-No.2.pdf accessed on 09 May 24

13 https://www.dawn.com/trends/raddul-fasaad accessed on 09 May 24.
14 https://tribune.com.pk/story/1336206/upsurge-terror-army-mounts-new-nationwide-offensive accessed on 23 Apr 24
15 https://ihl-databases.icrc.org/en/national-practice/protection-pakistan-act-2014 accessed on 10 May 25.
16 Fair C. Christine, Obama's New "Af-Pak" Strategy: Can "Clear, Hold, Build, Transfer" Work?, The Centre for International Governance Innovation Paper, 2010, https://ciaotest.cc.columbia.edu/wps/cigi/0022411/f_0022411_18465.pdf accessed on 10 May 24.
17 Nawaz Shuja, Learning by Doing, The Pakistan Army's Experience with Counterinsurgency, p. 18. https://www.files.ethz.ch/isn/126743/020111_ACUS_Nawaz_PakistanCounterinsurgency.pdfaccessed on 10 Jan 24.
18 https://shujanawaz.com/2011/02/learning-by-doing-the-pakistan-armys-experience-with-counterinsurgency/ accessed on 10 May 25.
19 Ibid.
20 Maheen Shafeeq, An Introduction to Converged Battle Domains (CBD) for Pakistan's Defence Forces, Centre for Aerospace & Security Studies, Islamabad, Pakistan. https://casstt.com/an-introduction-to-converged-battle-domains-cbd-for-pakistans-defence-forces/ accessed on 24 Apr 24.
21 Abbas, Hassan. Pakistan's Drift into Extremism: Allah, the Army, and America's War on Terror. Armonk, NY: M.E. Sharpe, 2005.
22 Bokhari, Farhan. "Pakistan's Military Develops Homegrown Drone for Counterterrorism." Financial Times, March 15, 2015. https://www.ft.com.
23 Raza, Ali. "Pakistan's Use of UAVs: Indigenous Progress and Future Prospects." Pakistan Institute for Peace Studies (PIPS) Report, 2021. https://www.pakpips.com.
24 Pakistan Space and Upper Atmosphere Research Commission (SUPARCO). Annual Progress Report 2020. Islamabad: Government of Pakistan, 2021.
25 https://www.eurasiareview.com/25012022-pakistan-and-national-cyber-command-a-strategic-competitive-enabler-part-i-oped/ accessed on 04 May 25.
26 Shah, Saeed. "How Pakistan Uses Chinese Tech to Monitor its Citizens." The Wall Street Journal, July 10, 2020. https://www.wsj.com.
27 Yusuf, Moeed. "Safe Cities and Surveillance: Pakistan's Quiet Embrace of AI." Brookings Institution, May 12, 2022. https://www.brookings.edu.
28 National Counter Terrorism Authority (NACTA). National Internal Security Policy 2018–2023. Islamabad: Ministry of Interior, 2018. https://nacta.gov.pk.Federal Investigation Agency (FIA). Cyber Crime Annual Report 2021. Islamabad: Ministry of Interior. https://fia.gov.pk.
29 Jones, Seth G., et al. Counterterrorism and the Role of Special Operations Forces. Santa Monica, CA: RAND Corporation, 2017.
30 Rashid Maria. 2021. *Dying to Serve: Militarism, Affect, and the Politics of Sacrifice in the Pakistan Army*. Lahore: Folio Books (Pakistan Edition), p. 56.
31 The Legacy of Lal Masjid, https://www.dawn.com/news/1344098 accessed on 01 Apr 23.

32 https://www.poetryfoundation.org/poems/46560/dulce-et-decorum-est accessed on 04 May 24.
33 Rashid, pp. 180-181.
34 Ibid, p. 204.
35 Rashid, Ahmed.Taliban: Militant Islam, Oil and Fundamentalism in Central Asia. Yale University Press, 2000, p. 129.
36 https://www.newindianexpress.com/nation/2025/Apr/29/hashim-musa-ex-pakistan-army-special-forces-soldier-prime-suspect-in-pahalgam-terror-attack accessed on 04 May 25.
37 ChristineC Fair, Fighting to the End: The Pakistan Army's Way of War. Oxford University Press, 2014, p. 83.
38 Huma Yusuf, "Radicalization and the Pakistan Army." United States Institute of Peace, October 2012.
39 Rana, Muhammad Amir. "Radicalization of Pakistan Navy." Dawn, September 13, 2014.
40 https://www.voanews.com/a/two-pakistani-army-officers-given-death-jail-sentences-for-espionage-/4938841.html accessed on 04 May 25.
41 Seth GJones, Pakistan's Dangerous Game: The ISI and Support to Terrorism. RAND Corporation, 2016. Pg 59.
42 "Suicide Blast Kills Army's Surgeon General." Dawn, February 26, 2008.
43 ChristineC Fair, Fighting to the End: The Pakistan Army's Way of War. Oxford University Press, 2014. Pg 121.
44 Huma Yusuf, "Radicalization and the Pakistan Army." United States Institute of Peace, October 2012.
45 DeclanWalsh, *The Nine Lives of Pakistan: Dispatches from a Precarious State*. New York: W.W. Norton & Company, 2020. Pg 120.
46 https://www.orfonline.org/expert-speak/angry-army-defiant-imran accessed on 04 May 25.
47 https://www.reuters.com/world/asia-pacific/pakistan-armys-top-3-officers-sacked-over-attacks-by-ex-pm-khan-supporters-army-2023-06-26/ accessed on 04 May 25.
48 https://www.aljazeera.com/news/2024/12/10/pakistans-military-charges-former-spy-chief-over-political-activities accessed on 02 May 25.
49 https://www.cnbctv18.com/world/pakistans-army-chief-faces-ultimatum-resign-or-risk-military-coup-19579927.htm accessed on 04 May 25.
50 https://theorg.com/org/fauji-foundation-group accessed on 27 Jun 24.
51 Siddiqa Ayesha, Military Inc: Inside Pakistan's Military Economy, Pluto Press, London, 2007.
52 https://www.uts.edu.au/news/2023/05/explainer-pakistans-powerful-military-enterprise accessed on 04 May 25.
53 https://bharatshakti.in/the-rise-of-asim-bajwa-his-family-business-empire/ accessed on 04 May 25.
54 50 Commercial Entities being run by Armed Forces, https://www.dawn.com/news/1272211 accessed on 28 Mar 23.
55 Ibid, p. 153.
56 www.fauji.org.pk/investors_fin.php accessed on 30 Mar 23.

57 https://www.eurasiantimes.com/pakistan-army-set-to-get-full-control-of-60-billion-china-pakistan-economic-corridor-cpec/ accessed on 02 May 25.

58 Ibid.

59 https://www.satp.org/terrorism-update/62-people-working-on-the-cpec-project-were-killed-in-last-four-years-says-federal-interior-ministry accessed on 02 May 25.

60 https://www.aninews.in/news/world/asia/china-puts-pressure-on-islamabad-keen-on-its-own-security-companies-for-cpec-projects20220707232420/ accessed on 04 May 25.

61 https://economictimes.indiatimes.com/news/defence/what-is-azm-e-istehkam-pakistans-new-military-operation-tasked-to-take-on-ttp-and-other-militant-groups/articleshow/111280481.cms?from=mdr accessed on 04 May 25.

62 https://www.weforum.org/stories/2018/10/guarding-the-silk-road-how-chinas-private-security-companies-are-going-global/ accessed on 10 May 25.

63 https://www.idsa.in/wp-content/uploads/2024/05/18-1_Devendra-Kumar.pdf accessed on 04 May 25.

64 https://awt.com.pk/business-units/askari-guards-private-limited accessed on 05 May 25.

65 Information collected from the website of Askari Guards, available at https://www. askariguards.com/, accessed on 04 May 25.

66 Paul Charon and Jean-Baptiste Jeangeìne Vilmer, Chinese Influence Operations: A Machiavellian Moment, Institute for Strategic Research, French Ministry of Armed Forces, 2021.

67 'China's Role in Myanmar's Internal Conflicts', USIP Senior Study Group Final Report No. 1, United States Institute of Peace, September 2018.

68 https://awt.com.pk/boardofdirector accessed on 04 May 25.

69 https://www.deccanherald.com/world/china-concerned-over-safety-of-its-citizens-in-pakistan-fm-qin-asks-bilawal-to-take-strong-security-measures-to-protect-them-1179680.html accessed on 24 Jun 24.

70 https://www.business-standard.com/external-affairs-defence-security/news/china-s-latest-demand-is-a-bitter-pill-to-swallow-for-pakistan-here-s-why-124060200665_1.html accessed on 23 Jun 24.

71 https://www.orfonline.org/research/azm-e-istehkam-china-s-wish-is-pakistan-s-command accessed on 27 Jun 24.

72 https://timesofindia.indiatimes.com/world/pakistan/under-pressure-from-china-will-pakistan-risk-war-with-the-taliban/articleshow/111338970.cms accessed on 30 Jun 24.

Five

Military Thought Driven by Culture

The Pakistan Army's approach to national security transcends the archaic *bullet versus butter* dialectic and aims at developing responses capable of tackling traditional and non-traditional security threats while keeping the idea of Pakistan as an Islamic welfare state paramount.[1] The Pakistan Army in all its articulation aspires to achieve peaceful coexistence, regional connectivity and shared prosperity in the region. The Pakistani military strategy predicates itself on the basic framework of ensuring citizens' safety, security, dignity and prosperity. As a vector of national power, the Pakistan armed forces believe that they must be able to mitigate the entire continuum of threats; traditional and non-traditional. The Pakistan Army is committed to safeguarding the sovereignty in all its manifestations in all domains of conflict including cyber, space and human cognition.

The Pakistan military thought is predicated on four pillars of pragmatism, proactiveness, prioritization and consistency.[2] The Pakistan Army is a professional army and executes its processes after due analysis of political aim in the light of guidelines provided by the security policy, identification and analysis of geo-political and operational environment. Identification of the nature of future wars has been a key driver towards its capability development and engagement with the other militaries in the region. Viewed through the lens of the decision makers in Rawalpindi, international politics is constantly evolving, mutating and presenting multiple challenges to Pakistan as the great powers are asserting themselves in the race for resources, power and influence in the world order where Pakistan finds it stifled and pushed to a corner. The militarization of global commons has led to New Revolution in Mil Affairs (NRMA)[3] with renewed competition for military domination. While the Pakistan Army had perfected the art of sub-conventional warfare, the recent conflicts have revived the concept of inter-state wars which invariably has forced the Pakistan Army to recalibrate its military thought. Pakistan, since its inception, has capitalized on the geo-economically pivotal geography that affords it the ability to offer itself as a bridge between civilizations and a melting pot of regional and global economic interests.[4] Stephen P. Cohen states, "*Something or someone will always come to Pakistan's rescue because of its location.*"[5] The historical, ethnic and religious ties across its western borders in Iran and Afghanistan have created externalities wherein peace and stability must have a positive influence on internal security. However, the same has been vitiated by the revival of a separatist movement in Baluchistan and fundamentalist groups like TTP, Jundullah and AQ challenging the sovereignty of the state.

The Pakistan Army's primary and existential adversary remains India which it believes will never ever accept the existence of Pakistan as an entity. The resolution of the Kashmir dispute remains a paramount national security interest and like it was said by General Asim Munir in his much commented speech on '*the jugular vein*,'[6] the Pakistan Army believes that by abrogation of Article 370, India has unilaterally changed the status quo in August 2019 in Jammu and Kashmir and has further exacerbated the path to resolution by steps taken from 2019 to 2025. The emerging Indo-US strategic convergence is further complicating the landscape of geopolitics for Pakistan in the Indo-Pacific particularly against them. In reaction, Pakistan has also tailored a '*full spectrum deterrence*'[7] strategy against India fearing that any further fluctuations in the balance of power equation would enhance the probability of a catastrophic war. The growing proximity of the USA and India has pushed Pakistan further into the Chinese circle of influence and while the technology and financial support to Pakistan by China is well documented, over a period of time the orientation of the officer corps of the Pakistan military, which had since independence relied on US and Europe's professional military education, doctrines and processes, has transcended to a more Sino-centric approach to war and war-fighting.

Regular bilateral exercises, such as the '*Warrior*'[8] '*Sea Guardians*'[9] and '*Shaheen*'[10] series of exercises, enhance interoperability and mutual understanding. These exercises increasingly feature complex operational scenarios involving information warfare, anti-submarine operations and network-centric warfare, reflecting evolving military doctrines. Hundreds of Pakistani officers train in Chinese military academies, absorbing not just tactics but also strategic thinking influenced by China's People's Liberation Army (PLA). China increasingly exploits military education as a method of promoting its model of governance, military culture as well as ideological education. China's 'Party-Army model' is a hard sell and tends to 'reinforce elite networks and hierarchies, which in China often supersede institutional and constitutional procedures.'[11] The PLA model is more synchronous with crony-capitalism and the civil-military corporatism of the Pak MILBUS and the hybrid model of control of the state through military means. Three tiers of military education for Pakistani officers in China have been identified. Students at all tiers can expect to receive ideological training in the Chinese Party-Army relations model. First, regional academies for cadets and junior officers, which include the PLA Air Force Aviation University; and second, command and staff colleges include the Army Command College and Command and Staff Colleges of PLA service branches. Most Pakistani military officers train at these levels; and third, the upper tier includes the National Defence University and National University of Defence Technology (NUDT).[12] The Army Command College is administered by the PLA and based in Nanjing. Beyond its use as an academy for commanders in the PLA ground forces, it hosts students from foreign countries, recently including those from Gambia and Pakistan. The college was among the first group of military academies to provide long-term military training courses for foreign officers, which it has done since 1957. Most of the college's training of foreign military officers takes place at the International Military Education Exchange Centre (IMEEC), created in 1957 and originally a classified organisation which is overseen by the Army Command College.[13] The IMEEC submits its own training plans to the joint staff department of the Central Military Commission (CMC), the headquarters of the PLA (until 2016 known as the PLA general staff headquarters): once these are approved, countries around the world may select officers for enrolment. The education of foreign officers, part of what China calls 'military political work' has emerged as a key area of Chinese engagement. 'Military political work' (junduizhengzhigongzuo; 军队政治工作)[14] describes all the activities of the China's People's Liberation Army (PLA) to shape the civilian environment to achieve the political, ideological, and military objectives set by the Chinese Communist Party (CCP).[15] These include political and ideological consciousness-raising across the force, public affairs and 'United Front work' (to mobilize support from outside the party), and educational functions like Professional Military Education (PME).

While the militaries of Pakistan and China come from different historical traditions, Pakistan's military culture has deep roots in British colonial legacies, and China's PLA is grounded in revolutionary Marxist ideology; despite this, their proximity has led to a growing cultural convergence. Both militaries emphasize on asymmetric strategies to counter superior conventional adversaries (India for Pakistan; the USA and its allies for China).

Pakistan's adoption of Chinese drones, missile technology and cyber capabilities mirrors China's broader philosophy of overcoming qualitative disadvantages through technological innovation. Inspired by Chinese concepts of integrated joint operations and informationized warfare, Pakistan is increasingly focusing on network-centric and multi-domain operations. Like China's approach to protracted struggle and incremental gains (e.g., in the South China Sea), Pakistan's military has adopted a doctrine of strategic patience, especially in handling its eastern and western borders.

The key factor in Pakistan's gravitation to China is its disappointment with the USA. Specifically, this shift began after the US's unilateral actions inside Pakistan during the global war on terrorism. The bilateral relationship was irreversibly damaged when US Navy SEALs conducted a heliborne raid in Abbottabad and killed Osama bin Laden in May 2011 and a NATO strike that killed 24 Pakistani soldiers on a check-post bordering Afghanistan.[16] The Pakistani military was rattled by the strikes and unacceptable aggression without prior information. Pakistan's response to the American raid was twofold; first, they demanded a review of the partnership with Washington in the fight against terrorism and Pakistan began to look towards China as a potential security partner, seeking to develop a partnership similar to the one it has had with the USA since the 1950s.[17]

More recently, a trove of US secrets has been published by US media outlets, providing evidence that Pakistan relies heavily on Chinese investments and loans and that its officials are reconsidering their relationships with both China and America.[18] The documents offered a unique insight into Pakistan's internal deliberations as it navigated the choppy waters of a changing global landscape, where the status of the USA as a super power was under scrutiny. The leaked internal memos also contain two warnings to policymakers not to anger China in their efforts to maintain relations with the USA. In one of the memos, titled 'Pakistan's Difficult Choices,' Hina Rabbani Khar, Pakistan's erstwhile minister of state for foreign affairs, argues that Pakistan is no longer able to sustain a neutral position between China and the USA. She cautions against appeasing the West and instead argues that sustaining Pakistan's alliance with the USA would ultimately mean giving up the advantages of its 'actual strategic partnership with China.'[19] It offers crucial insights into the complex geopolitical calculations of Pakistan and the challenges facing the USA as it seeks to maintain its global influence. As some observers of Islamabad's calculation maintain, "It is unclear who will end up in the pole position in 10 years' time, so they need to diversify their risks and hedge their bets."[20]

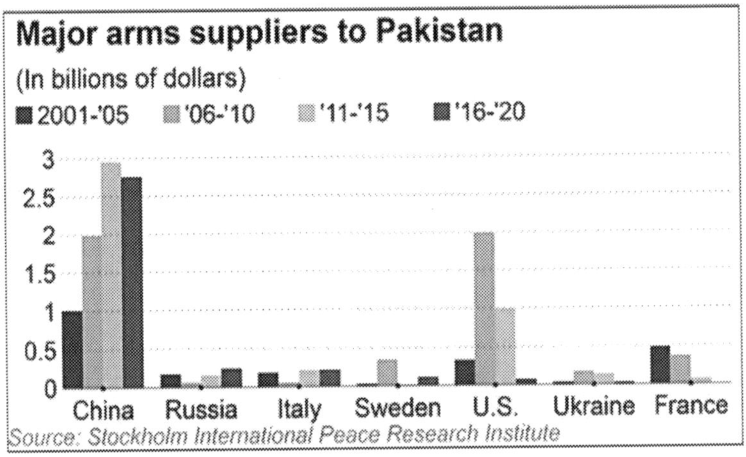

Fig. 18: Pakistan Import of Arms

The deep-rooted historic ties between China and Pakistan are driven by shared interests and mutual understanding. China's position as a champion of shared economic growth and mutual benefit is inextricably tied to the BRI with CPEC as its cornerstone. Pakistan's economic travails notwithstanding, China has remained an all-weather ally contributing to enhancing all vectors of Pakistan's national power. Chinese supplies in 2024 ramped up to 81 per cent of Pakistan's weapons imports according to data from the Swedish think tank SIPRI. That is a rise of seven percentage points from the previous five-year period to

2019, when 74 per cent of Pakistan's arms imports came from China.[21] The support of China during the C5 Continuum (Coop-Competition-Crisis-Confrontation-Conflict) is integral to Pakistan's strategic calculus and the relationship is a symbiotic one with Pakistan human resources and real estate providing the necessary impetus.

The most important link between the militaries of China and Pakistan is also economic; the 1,300-kilometre-long Karakoram Highway that was operationalized in 1982. Pakistan cold-tested a nuclear device and subsequently acquired blueprints for a nuclear bomb from China. Beijing supplied nuclear-capable missiles to Islamabad via the Karakoram Highway, besides outfitting the Pakistani army with conventional weaponry.[22] It is not surprising to note that this period coincided with the beginning of massive and systemic Pakistani support to insurgent groups in Punjab. The Karakoram Highway was crucial in augmenting the Pakistani military's strength and enabling Islamabad to pursue a covert war against India. Beginning in Punjab, this war expanded to Jammu and Kashmir (J&K) in 1989. Since then, Pakistan has lost all inhibitions about escalating hostilities through proxy warfare taking action even in the hinterland of India to prove to the world that the terrorism in India is home grown and that India is a polarized society.

Pakistan shares a deep fraternal relationship with all countries of the Middle East based on historical facts, mutual trust, symbiotic cooperation and long-standing economic ties. Deep ties with Saudi Arabia have been forged over the ages and Pakistan has totally committed to the safety of the two holiest sites of Islam. Historically, Muslims in the Indian sub-continent have inherited a rich legacy from the Persian civilisation and Sufi traditions. The poet Muhammad Iqbal did place the Arabian homeland, Hijaz, at the centre of his poetry when he wrote, for instance, "What does it matter if my wine jar is Persian? At least the wine is Arabian (Hijazi). What matters if the song is Indian (Hindi)? The tune, after all, is Arabian (Hijazi)." As president of the Muslim League, Chaudhury Khaliquzzaman argued in 1949 that "Pakistan would bring all Muslim countries together into Islamistan; a pan-Islamic entity."[23] In 1942, he had declared that "Pakistan is only the jumping off ground. The time is not distant when the Muslim countries will have to stand in line with Pakistan."[24] Initially, Saudi Arabia resented the manner in which Pakistan joined hands with the USA, the best friend of Israel, through its membership of the SEATO and CENTO. Riyadh initiated the Muslim World League and then the Organisation of Islamic Conference in the 1960s. In the wake of the 1971 war, Bhutto made overtures to Saudi Arabia because he had felt let down by the USA and China. Bhutto needed money to develop what was to be known as the 'Islamic' bomb.[25] This rapprochement was consolidated under General Zia-ul-Haq. His Islamisation policy (an emissary of Saudi King Faisal, Maruf Dualibi, 'framed' the 1980 Zakat and Ushr Ordinance)[26] and the anti-Soviet jihad in Afghanistan helped Zia in consolidating ties with Saudi Arabia, which not only matched the American financial support to Pakistan, but also helped it to develop Islamist networks from madrassas to jihadi groups such as the Lashkar-e-Taiba and the Haqqani network. The Saudis have continued to cultivate their constituency in Pakistan since then. As a result, they can rely on three kinds of friends within the country. They get the support of Islamists of different kinds; the Jamaat-e-Islami in the past and currently, the Deobandi and Ahl-e-Hadith groups, including the Lashkar-e-Taiba, whose leader, Hafiz Saeed, was trained in Saudi Arabia. These groups and madrassas benefit from funding by Saudi charities.

Besides these links, Saudi Arabia remained the largest source of workers' remittances to Pakistan, contributing $ 728.3 million in January 2025, according to the State Bank of Pakistan (SBP).[27] This marked a significant 25.2 per cent rise in remittances compared to the previous months, a vital lifeline for Pakistan's economy, which has been grappling with an ongoing economic crisis.[28] Saudi Arabia and Pakistan fight the al-Qaeda and ISIS together, but cultivate 'their' separate Islamists. The Pakistan Army sees its relationship with Saudi Arabia as special, owing to its persistent economic crisis. Pakistan has been economically dependent on Saudi Arabia. The kingdom has come to Pakistan's rescue on many occasions; for example when Pakistan was under international economic sanctions during 1998–2001 because of testing its nuclear weapons in May 1998. Then, Saudi Arabia provided oil support to Pakistan, calling the gesture 'a gift in times of need.'[29] In 2009, Riyadh granted Pakistan a loan of US$ 380 million and a gift of US$ 300 million at the Tokyo Donor Conference to help ease high oil prices.[30] From 2014 to 2022, Pakistan received three Saudi financial aid packages totalling nearly US$ 9.5 billion.[31] During 2005–2022, Pakistan was among the top five beneficiaries of the King Salman Humanitarian Aid and Relief Centre which had implemented projects worth US$ 146.9 million in the country.[32] From 1975 to 2021, the top 10 recipients of Saudi Arabia's overseas development assistance included nine majority Muslim states and Palestine.[33] During this period, Pakistan was the fourth largest recipient of aid after Yemen, Syria, and Palestine.

Religious groups, including Islamists in Pakistan like the Jamaat-e-Islami, have been traditionally inspired by Saudi Arabia. During the 1980s, the Jamaat was a key ally of General Zia-ul-Haq in terms of promoting Islamization inspired by Saudi Arabia or Sunni Wahhabi Islam.[34] The kingdom has long been a major centre for Islamic scholarship and has invested heavily in promoting Islamic education in Pakistan. Saudi Arabia enjoys a multifaceted influence on education, especially religious education in Pakistan. There are many facets of that including the impact on madrassas, public sector schools and universities. Saudi Arabia's funding before the 1980s was mainly towards building mosques and madrassas in Pakistan but this shifted towards the promotion of anti-Shi'a ideology during the 1980s.[35] While the kingdom has always enjoyed a special place among Pakistani Muslims, Riyadh was offered an important opportunity during the Afghan-Soviet War (1979–1988) to expand its ideological influence in Pakistan. Then Pakistan and Saudi Arabia sided with the USA and promoted jihad (holy war) against the Soviet invasion of Afghanistan. A prominent madrassa in Pakistan's north-west, Dar-ul Ulum Haqqania, had a visible acknowledgement of Saudi funding as it has a plaque mentioning that it was built as a gift from the Kingdom of Saudi Arabia.[36] As reported by Rahman,[37] Ahle Hadith madrassas in Pakistan rely heavily on Arabic books published and printed in Saudi Arabia. Saudi Arabia has been promoting its religious ideology and culture in Pakistan. The kingdom has a generous scholarship scheme for Muslim students. The scholarship scheme for Pakistan is quite targeted as it mainly focuses on religious studies and excludes degree programs in other disciplines like health and medicine. In 2021, Saudi Arabia announced 600 scholarships for Pakistan, compared to 583 in 2019.[38] Since 1978, Islamic Studies has been a compulsory subject at all levels of education up to the first degree, including professional qualifications. On the website of Higher Education of Pakistan, 236 degree-awarding institutions are listed.[39] Hence naturally, there is a significant demand for graduates of Islamic Studies, especially graduates from Saudi universities. In its efforts to gain influence in Pakistan, for geopolitical gains vis-à-vis Iran, Saudi Arabia has historically been promoting Salafism. As mentioned above, not all of the kingdom's cultural influence is benign as Pakistan continues to suffer from radicalization and extremism that had mainly started through the establishment of Saudi-funded madrassas in the 1980s; extremism is Saudi Arabia's top export to Pakistan.[40]

The military partnership between Saudi Arabia and Pakistan traces its origins back to 1967 when a significant defence agreement was inked primarily focusing on the training of the Royal Armed Forces of KSA.[41] This landmark agreement commenced an uninterrupted exchange of defence expertise, strategic planning, training and equipment from Pakistan to KSA. In the 1960s, Pakistani pilots operated RSAF fighter jets during

Saudi Arabia's conflict with Yemen, known as the al-Wadiah conflict, as the PAF supported the RSAF (established in 1969).[42] The Pakistan Army played a pivotal role in assisting Saudi authorities in resolving the 1979 Grand Mosque seizure. Saudi Arabia has traditionally considered Pakistan an ally, particularly in matters of security. In the 1980s, Saudi Arabia relied on Pakistan, deploying 15,000 soldiers for its defence. During the first Gulf War, 13,000 Pakistani military personnel actively participated. Earlier, Pakistani Army engineers had constructed fortifications along the Saudi-Yemen border. Currently, approximately 1,800 Pakistani officers and soldiers are serving in Saudi Arabia as part of a military training mission.[43] Thousands of members of the Royal Saudi Armed Forces have also received training in Pakistan, and both countries frequently conduct joint military exercises. The exchange of ideas and ideology has led to the proliferation of the Salafi thought process within the Pakistan military. In the past the Pakistan military had played the Islam card often but also was aware where to draw the line as far as conduct of military activities was concerned. Pakistan and Saudi Arabia were both key US partners in the Afghan-Soviet War, but the former's role was much bigger in terms of the recruitment and mobilization of fighters (mujahideen) to defeat the Soviet troops in Afghanistan. Saudi Arabia's funding played a key role in terms of promoting conservative Salafi ideology in South Asia and laid the foundations for violent religious extremism. The cooperation between Saudi Arabia and Pakistan was visibile even when Pakistan's former army chief Raheel Sharif was appointed first commander-in chief of a new counterterrorism coalition of 39 Islamic countries in 2017.[44] The Salafi strain within the military grew manifold due to close interaction between the Saudi Royal Army and the Pakistan military. "Until the late 1970s, mosques located at armed forces bases (i.e., Army, Air Force and Navy) were 90 per cent Ahle Sunnat Wal Jama't (Sufi), 8 per cent Deobandi, and zero per cent Salafi. Currently, 85 per cent of the mosques are

Deobandi or Salafi, and less than 10 per cent are Ahle Sunnat Wal Jama't,"[45] a clear indicator of the expansion of Salafi radical ideology within the military. Religiosity in the armed forces has assumed different forms; a cultural tilt towards religion; an active radicalism; and anti-American nationalism. In other words, the manifestations of religiosity have become so variegated and so strongly linked to the national and international politics of the day that there can be no single or simple method to do something about them.

Pakistan recently has fallen out of favour in West Asia, especially Gulf Cooperation Council (GCC) countries; its relations with Afghanistan, Saudi Arabia and Iran have worsened leading Pakistani leaders to turn to Türkiye to offer a new narrative to their people. The Turkic connection with the Mughal dynasty was the starting point of this affiliation. The inclination of the Muslim populace in the subcontinent toward Türkiye arose in 1919, when the 'Khilafat Movement' to defend the Caliph was launched under the leadership of Shaukat Ali and Maulana Abul Kalam Azad. In 1920, the Indian National Congress supported the contention and it was this recognition of the ruler of the Ottoman Empire as the Khalifa of Muslims in the subcontinent that laid the foundation of modern Pakistan's relationship with Islamised Türkiye under President Erdogan. The Urdu language incorporates Persian, Hindi, Arabic and Turkish vocabulary, highlighting Turkic integration into the region's culture.[46] Extending this cultural and societal association in recent times has been the popular TV show, Ertugrul,[47] that transmits the religious populism of Erdogan. The show is a prime example of Türkiye's soft power, allowing them to transmit the narrative of 'Islamist civilisationalism,'[48] rooted in glorification of the Turkic ethnicity and positioning themselves as guardians of the Ummah.[49] The hallmark of populism are two homogeneous and antagonistic groups; 'the pure people' versus 'the corrupt elite.'[50] The show plays on this dichotomy, allowing Pakistan to feel that a part of the Muslim Ummah has been victimized by the whims of the 'Western world'. Erdogan and his party have hooked the willing Pakistani populace suffering from a perpetual ontological crisis.[51] The vertical and horizontal divides[52] within Pakistan are also cemented through the show's themes. The vertical dimension of Islamic populism divides the 'Ummah; versus the 'others,' represented by the Western countries, Jews, Indians, Armenians, etc., while the horizontal dimension marks the Ummah as the 'true people' due to their celestial superiority (Islamism) against the 'evil' or 'godless' others. Civilizational populism is intertwined with faith, superseding plain nationalism to civilizationism.

Turkey has used its transnational civilizationism to not only expand its relations with Pakistan but also muster support during the Nagorno-Karabakh war. While Pakistan did not officially declare its military involvement in the conflict, troops supported the Türkiye-backed army in Azerbaijan along with sympathetic statements of support for Azerbaijan.[53] Türkiye, Azerbaijan and Pakistan share a transnational relationship that makes them the Ummah against the 'infidels.' On the domestic level, Ertugrul Ghazi (TV show) has ensured cultural convergence of the societies that are beyond the show and have more permanent features. The long-term cultural ties feature not only telecasting more Islamized Turkish shows but also jointly produced television shows like, Lala Turki.[54] Retail brands in Pakistan are now using slogans such as 'uniting cultures' and 'Muslim heritage' to sell their merchandise in a market where Turkishness is the new fad.[55] The name of Istanbul reminds them of the Hagia Sophia, that was just 'reconquered' by the Erdogan government and re-converted to a mosque.[56] Istanbul Chowk now represents the land of the 'true' and 'fierce' Muslims. Pakistan has pitched in for solidifying transnational Islamist populism promulgated by the Erdogan regime. Ankara, Islamabad and Kuala Lumpur, with Qatar as an additional partner, have constituted an emergent power nexus, built around a common orientation towards a conservative, Sunni political Islam. This nexus is united as much by common enmities as by common affections. Its enemies are

India, Israel and at the rhetorical level, the Christian West. Its rivals within the Islamic world are Saudi Arabia, which has traditionally dominated the OIC, the main pan-Islamic diplomatic body. The crystallization of this new alliance has been apparent for some time.[57]

In the 21st century, defence ties between Turkey and Pakistan have grown stronger than ever, reflecting an alignment in both strategic needs and military culture. Turkey is building MILGEM-class corvettes for Pakistan under a major defence deal, with technology transfer agreements allowing Pakistani shipyards to co-produce. Regular joint exercises like the 'Atatürk' series and 'Jinnah' focus on counter-terrorism, amphibious operations and special operations training. Turkish military academies host many Pakistani cadets and officers and vice versa, building a shared operational ethos. The convergence between Turkish and Pakistani militaries extends beyond equipment and drills to shared ways of thinking; both militaries consciously preserve Islamic values in their operational and organizational culture, which, under President Erdogan's leadership, has revived Islamic motifs within the traditionally secular Turkish Armed Forces (TSK). The militaries of both nations promote values like martyrdom (*shahadat*), jihad in defence of the homeland, and moral discipline, strengthening cultural bonds. Turkish Special Forces (Özel Kuvvetler) and Pakistan's SSG (Special Services Group) have similar operational philosophies focusing on speed, agility, and deep insertion missions. Their counter-terrorism, mountain warfare and urban warfare training modules mirror each other's tactical preferences. This shared experience has led both militaries to emphasize self-reliance, domestic defence industries, and indigenous technological innovation.

Pakistan has an enduring relationship with the EU and UK and has endeavoured to keep this partnership going even after BREXIT. Increased cooperation in the domains of trade, connectivity, security and people-to-people interaction is predicated on a sizeable and influential Diaspora on both sides of the English Channel. Multilateral cooperation with the EU and single-nation interactions in Europe has been mutually beneficial. Pakistan has emerged as one of the most prominent contributors to the Ukrainian war effort under the arrangement of the Ukraine Security Asst Initiative (USAI).[58]

Amn	Qty	Funds
155 mm How	60,000	364 mn $ recd
309 mn $ pending		
120 mm Mor	25,000	
122 mm HE	20,000	
122 mm MBRL Rkt	130,000	
40 mm RPG HEAT	30,000	

Fig. 19: Ammunition Support to Ukraine

The Pakistan Army will continue to champion the cause of the Ummah and Muslim inclusivity. The Pakistan military is committed to stand firmly against Islamophobia and support the proliferation of Islam as it has become visible in Bangladesh. The aim of Pakistan in the comity of nations would be to take an 'independent principled position' to leverage its geo-strategic location and develop relationships with all other Muslim countries based on 'mutual respect and sovereign equality'.

Role of the Pakistan Military and Fundamentals of Military Doctrine

The security of land, air, sea, cyber, space and ideological borders is the paramount responsibility of the Pakistan armed forces. The Pakistan Army claims to continue to pursue the concept of 'open and secure borders'[59] despite the stressors on both its eastern and western fronts. The Global War on Terror (GWOT) has brought to the fore the importance of the Pakistani armed forces, para military forces (PMF) and law enforcement agencies (LEA) in ensuring internal cohesion and assertion of state control within the geographical confines of the state. Special attention is required to manage lingering border disputes which can exacerbate the security situation and lead to a conflict in a nuclearized neighbourhood. With a regressive and dangerously polarized ideology gripping our neighbourhood, the prospects of the use of violence have grown immensely. Opportunities to consolidate the writ of rule and law in KPK and Baluchistan because of Op AZM-E-ISTEKAM[60] must not be missed. Border management and maintenance of peace along the Durand Line and the Goldsmith Line are critical to promoting trade and ensuring regional security for the Pakistan military.

Under Article 245 of the Constitution of the Islamic Republic of Pakistan, 1973, as modified up to 31 May 2018,[61] the Rules of Business 1973 have been framed and under Schedule-II of the same, the Ministry of Defence (Defence Division) is responsible for defence of the Federation or any part of thereof in peace or war. The defence policy of Pakistan was approved by the defence committee on 9 March 2004 that postulates the framework for ensuring the territorial integrity of Pakistan through defence and deterrence capability. Post the departure of the USA from Afghanistan, the regional scenario has undergone a cataclysmic shift and has led to a change in the security priorities of Pakistan. The unsettled Durand Line has direct a linkage with the Pakistani armed forces and has a domino effect on the capacity and capability on the eastern front of Pakistan. The policy framework[62] of the Pakistan Army is to defend its borders based on credible deterrence predicated on conventional military strength and nuclear capability backed by a united nation appreciative of the values for which the armed forces stand. The Pakistani armed forces will aspire to follow a policy of combination of war avoidance, deterrence and defence based on a pragmatically worked-out confluence of military posture, strategic weapon disposition, conventional response matrix and suitable response in the continuum of conflict. The fundamentals of Pakistan's military doctrine are based on the historical past; institutional belief system and experience; ethos and principles of the military. The doctrine provides a philosophical foundation from which the thinking begins. It provides ways to use military means against a given type of threat or scenario and has implications for force structure, training and equipment.[63] The ideal military doctrine should be truly joint, integrating land, air, maritime, cyber, space and special operations in an effective way to achieve the military objective.

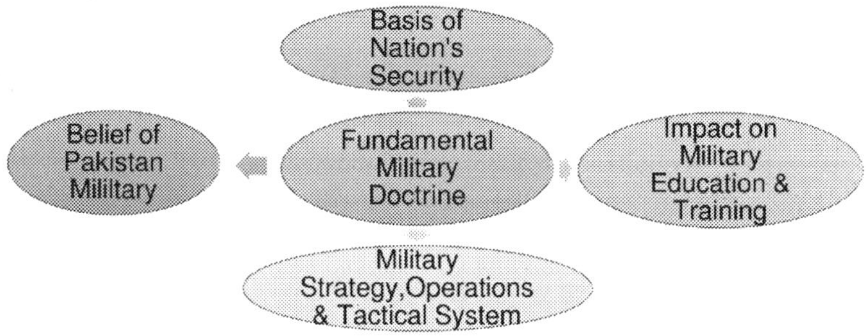

Fig. 20: Effect of Military Doctrine

For Pakistan, the Quran places war-fighting doctrine and its theory in a much different category than what others are accustomed to because it is not a theory of war derived by man, but of God and it is his war-fighting principles and commandments as revealed to a true Muslim. The Quranic approach to war is "infinitely supreme and effective and points towards the realization of universal peace and justice. It makes maximum allowance to its adversaries to cooperate with Islam in a combined search for a just and peaceful order."[64] Zia-ul-Haq focused on the concept of jihad in Islam and explaining it as not simply the domain of the military; *Jehad fi sabilallah*[65] is not the exclusive domain of the professional soldier, nor is it restricted to the application of military force alone. "In Islam war is waged to establish supremacy of the Lord only when every other argument has failed to convince those who reject his will and work against the very purpose of the creation of mankind."[66] Regarding modernization and transformation, all modern techniques which are not foreign to this concept can be accommodated while working out the details.[67] The Pakistan Army sought the effective coordination and support of other vectors of national power and law enforcement agencies to deal with insurgency. Military operations have substantially aggrieved the local population and have led to deterioration of the overall security situation in the country. Continuous Intelligence Based Operations (IBO)[68] supported by modern weapons and equipment has however helped forge a battle-hardened force capable of operating in the entire spectrum of operations.

Pakistan's fundamental military doctrine has always been Islamic in approach. Part of the army's legacy is the idea that any insult or slight must be avenged, not only to punish the aggression of the enemy but also to honour the sacrifices of the earlier generations. This serves as a motivational strategy against India. Nothing much has changed with respect to the usage of Islam as an important ingredient of the fundamental military doctrine. In a society that owes its existence to Islam, its adoption is inescapable; any other system based on borrowed concepts will never appeal to the heart and soul of a Muslim soldier. The armed forces cultivate a deep respect for the values of jihad which is evident in much of Pakistan's military literature as well. The Pakistan Army is not going to give up its use of jihad and mujahedeen as a strategic weapon against adversaries.

The logic behind having a nuclear capability is Indo-centric and the concept of a nuclear deterrence became a vital element of Pakistan's fundamental military doctrine. The nuclear dimension constitutes the most modern and advanced tenet in military doctrine. Pakistan's nuclear programme has a symbiotic relationship with India and provides Pakistan with an infrangible guarantee of its independence and physical integrity.[69] The Pakistan Army believes it places a limitation on violence and allows it to keep the threshold of conflict below total war as well as allows it to counter the conventional asymmetry of India.

Though a review of the doctrine has been done several times, the fundamentals have remained the same. Priority is still accorded to the creation of a sub-conventional warfare capability to fight domestically against non-state actors supporting sub-nationalism and ethnic and sectarian supremacy. Pakistan's fundamental military doctrine maintains its continuum since India will be painted as an existential threat. Until and unless this changes, the roots of its fundamental military doctrine will only go deeper and deeper. The Pakistani Army will never let its interest be at stake and hence, the roots of Pakistan's fundamental military doctrine remain strongly anti-India or anti-Hindustan. Owing to the legacy of belligerence, a lingering core issue like Kashmir, territorial sensitivities, internal vulnerability, Pakistan's security has multifarious challenges. Despite unfavourable and hostile conditions on the western borders, the Pakistan armed forces have always been able to bring back the focus of their mandate on defending the country's sovereignty against India. The threat of conventional and nuclear is adroitly balanced in land, air, maritime and cognitive domains against superiority in numbers 'to deny India the much-craved space for limited war'.[70] Pakistan's doctrinal success lies in utilizing full spectrum strategic deterrence to avoid an arms race with India, while equitably maintaining core military capability and exploit non-state actors to foment trouble in India. The threat to Pakistan as it is painted by their army is not so much of physical borders but of '*Nazariya-e-Pakistan*'[71] and that is to protect the ideology of Pakistan from India's Hindu identity. Islamic credentials and nuclear capability coupled with unsettled borders and unfinished agenda of Partition are considered triggers that can precipitate a conflict between Pakistan and India. Economic fragility and dependence on Bretton Woods Institutes has allowed the Western powers to engage in economic coercion which has further moved Pakistan closer to China.

Non-traditional security threats are challenges to the survival and well-being of people and states that arise primarily out of non-military sources, such as climate change, resource scarcity, infectious diseases, natural disasters, irregular migration, food shortages, people smuggling, drug trafficking and transnational crime. These dangers defy unilateral remedies and require comprehensive political, economic, social responses, as well as humanitarian use of military force. There are immense challenges of provincial discord accentuated by the floods of 2022 which has further degraded the economic capability of some provinces. Food scarcity along with water scarcity has led to migration of people to major cities creating a law-and-order challenge in urban areas. Today, Pakistan is considered one of the most water-stressed countries in the world. And 2024 was one of the driest in the country's history, with the Pakistan Meteorological Department reporting 67% less rainfall than usual. According to the Germanwatch 2025 Climate Risk Index, Pakistan ranked as the most vulnerable country to the impacts of climate change.[72] The impact of floods in 2022 have created a permanent damage of agricultural land and the data of the same is listed in Figure 20 below. The maximum production of agro products from the existing land parcel will still not be adequate to meet the requirements of the booming demographic profile of Pakistan as evident in Fig. 21 below.

ID	Province	Total agricultural area using land cover 2021 (km²)	Flooded agricultural area (km²)	Flooded agricultural area percentage (%)
1	Balochistan	33 750	4 972	15
2	Punjab	127 511	10 989	9
3	Sindh	52 981	19 436	37
4	Khyber Pakhtunkhwa	18 481	2 892	16
	Total	232 723	38 289	16

Fig. 21: Effect of Flooding on Provinces

thousand MT per Hectare					
			Required Yield		
Yield	Population growth (%)	Max. Yield achieved	2020	2030	2040
Wheat	1.8	2.973	2.7	3.3	3.9
	2.1		2.8	3.4	4.2
	2.4		2.8	3.5	4.5
Sugarcane	1.8	61.972	48.9	58.4	69.9
	2.1		49.3	60.7	74.8
	2.4		49.8	63.1	80.0
Data source: Economic Survey of Pakistan					

Fig. 22: Food Scarcity by 2040

The floods notwithstanding, Pakistan is becoming a water-starved state that would damage the societal fabric of the nation. The failure of Pakistan to harness the rivers and groundwater has been further exacerbated by injudicious construction of dams and barrages. As political instability, economic uncertainty, and climate shocks consume Islamabad's policy bandwidth, another long-term challenge remains neglected; Pakistan's water crisis. Unequal access to clean water is deepening existing socio-economic disparities and holds the potential to catalyse civil unrest amid macro-economic instability. Aging infrastructure, weak water governance, and the unpredictable impact of climate shocks could solidify water security as a threat multiplier for the state and society. Elite interests tied to water-intensive agriculture stymie the reforms necessary to address structural fault lines in the political economy that perpetuate water insecurity. Also, complicating reform efforts have uncertain political timelines with a lack of policy continuity from one government to the next. International lenders, meanwhile, have failed to prioritize water security when providing external assistance to Pakistan for decades. As a result, existing agricultural policies are geared towards maintaining the status quo by borrowing resources, both economic and water-related, from current and future generations.

A confluence of domestic and international factors suggests the current moment may offer an opportunity to address these enduring challenges. Water insecurity is likely to gain increasing domestic political salience as the impacts of climate change are felt by vast swaths of the country, which were seen most dramatically in the aftermath of the devastating floods in 2022. International financial institutions and foreign investors, meanwhile, are demanding demonstrable policy changes and greater accountability.[73] Without meaningful structural changes in Pakistan's agricultural sector, the water crisis will likely become one of the country's most consequential domestic challenges in going forward, with implications for broader regional stability. In rural Pakistan, the situation is particularly dire:

about 70 per cent of the population does not have access to clean drinking water, and 80 per cent lack adequate sanitation facilities.[74] This water scarcity is not merely a public health issue but a major economic burden as well. Managing water resources costs Pakistan nearly 4 per cent of its gross domestic product (GDP), amounting to approximately $ 12 billion annually, a figure that continues to grow as challenges intensify.[75]

Environmental degradation has further compounded the problem. In coastal districts such as Thatta and Badin, approximately 1.2 million acres of fertile land have been lost to sea erosion.[76] Each year, Pakistan loses an estimated 7 million acre-feet (MAF) of water to the Arabian Sea due to inadequate storage infrastructure and poor management practices. Despite being an agrarian economy that heavily depends on water, Pakistan's water reservoirs have a storage capacity of merely 30 days, far below the recommended international standard of 120 days. The human cost of this crisis is heart-rending. An estimated 53,000 children die every year from diseases caused by contaminated water.[77] Water-borne illnesses like diarrhoea, cholera and typhoid continue to plague communities, particularly those already marginalized by poverty and inadequate healthcare systems. The urgency is clear: without decisive and coordinated efforts, Pakistan risks facing a future where water scarcity could destabilize its economy, endanger its food security, and endanger millions of lives.

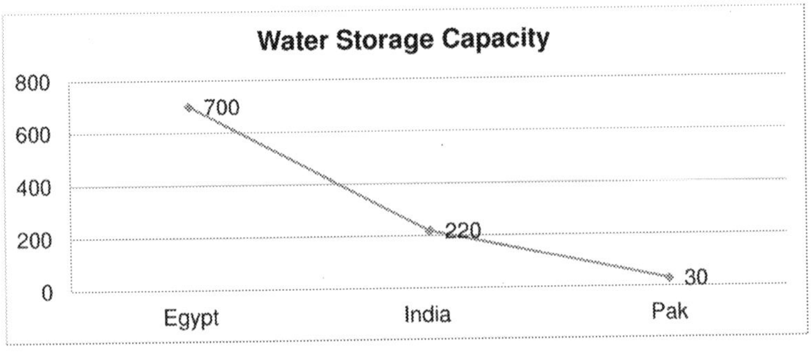

Fig. 23: Water Challenges for Pakistan[78]

Pakistan has one of the lowest literacy rates in the world and to further exacerbate the challenge, the population of Pakistan has grown exponentially. While Pakistan's constitution guarantees the right to education for all children aged 5 to 16, in practice, millions of children, particularly girls, do not attend school. The World Bank (2019) reported that nearly 22.8 million children in Pakistan are out of school, with the majority coming from poor rural households. A significant portion of Pakistan's poor are employed in the informal sector, which includes agriculture, construction and small-scale retail. According to the International Labour Organization (ILO, 2019), nearly 72% of workers in Pakistan are employed in informal jobs, which lack job security, benefits and legal protection.[79] These workers are particularly vulnerable to economic shocks, such as those caused by the COVID-19 pandemic and socio-economic stressors like feudalism which invariably leads to widespread job losses and wage cuts. Informal sector workers, including daily wage labourers, domestic workers, and street vendors, often earn barely enough to meet their basic needs. Without access to formal employment protections, such as pensions or healthcare benefits, they are at high risk of falling deeper into poverty during times of crisis and then resorting to unlawful means to make ends meet including joining terrorist groups not for reasons of religious radicalization but for making their ends meet. Civic amenities in urban centres have crumbled under human stress and corruption in governance has led to a large level of dissatisfaction with the political system. Brain drain and exodus of youth from the nation, both by legal and illegal means, has been a phenomenon indicative of deep-rooted dissatisfaction with the modus vivendi in Pakistan. The number of Pakistani refugees rose exceptionally from 49,000 in 2012 to 336,000 in 2013 and have been on the rise since then.[80] The population control measures in Pakistan have not had the desired effect with the decadal change in population of Pakistan second only to Nigeria in the world. The current assessment of the population situation in Pakistan points to the prevailing rapid population growth, amounting to 2.4 percent annually for the period (1998-2017) as was shown by the findings of the 2017 population census. The population of Pakistan increased six-fold during the period 1951-2017, from 34 million in 1951 to 208 million in 2017. This alarming trend is also expected to persist in the future; the United Nation's Population Division's medium projection shows that Pakistan's projected population will reach 263 million by 2030 and 383 million by 2050, i.e., an increase by about 84% during the 2017-2050 period,[81] unless serious actions are undertaken to halt population growth and rationalize population dynamics. Population pressure remains one of the leading factors behind lower per capita income, poor health and education outcomes, higher unemployment, inequality and dwindling of common resources in Pakistan.

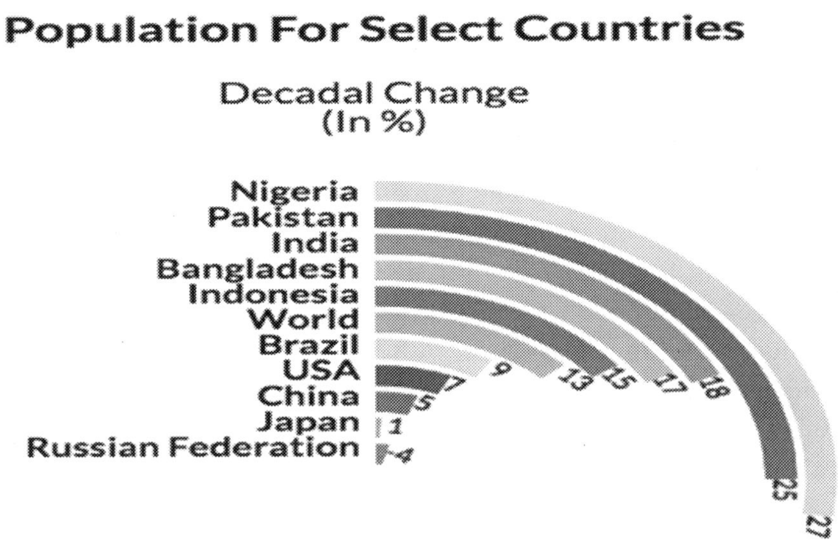

Fig. 24: Population Increase in Pakistan

The Pakistan Army culture is not quarantined from the societal stressors and the impact on its personnel by internal factors and also by external influences that shape the cognitive landscape of the decision makers. The transition from a US-based military education system to a PLA-driven curricula has created a new officer corps within the Pakistan armed forces which is not any more beholden to its Western minders and is willing to take more risks and at the same time buoyed by the unconditional support of China has upped the ante of sub-conventional warfare against India. It is also interesting to note that this marriage of convenience is between two diametrically opposite forces; an Islamic army which has jihad as part of its motto and a communist army for which the word 'religion' is taboo. The most in-your-face religious edict is what China has done in its Muslim province of Xinjiang by banning civil servants, students and teachers from fasting during Ramadan and ordering restaurants to stay open. This, in addition to earlier laws that Muslim men under 50 years of age cannot grow their beard to more than a certain length; women are not allowed to dress in too Islamic a way; mosques are monitored by anti-religious police, shows how very agnostic the Chinese really are with regard to religion.[82] The Islamic State of Pakistan, that champions the cause of Palestine, Kashmir and the Ummah, has not noticed any of this in its very close alliance with China. How has this been overlooked by Hafiz Saeed and organizations like Jud, Let and TLP, who are rather staunch Islamists. Perhaps even terrorists choose their fights carefully. They would rather attack a free country with millions of Muslims than help their troubled brethren in a Chinese province.

The effect of the CPEC on the Pakistan military has been profound, as the interaction of China has been less with the Pakistan federal government but more with the Pakistan Army to provide the requisite guarantees to the investment being made by Chinese government and MNCs. The targeting of CPEC projects by terrorist groups along the western borders and targeting of Chinese nationals during the recent past has put additional stress on the Pakistan military to come down on sub-nationalist groups with a heavy hand. The claims of Gen. Asim Munir of Pakistan to become a 'hard state' are defined by PLA intervention and persistent demands for the security apparatus for the CPEC to be revamped.

NOTES

1 https://static.theprint.in/wp-content/uploads/2022/01/NSP.pdf 5National Security Policy of Pakistan 2022-2026, p. 06. Accessed on 23 Apr 25.

2 Ibid, p. 09.

3 Dr. Zulfqar Khan, Military Strategies of India and Pakistan: A Perspective, p. 03. (Dr. Zulfqar Khan (Ph.D., MA University of Bradford; and post-graduation The Nottingham Trent University) is a professor of Strategic Studies & Director ORIC at the National Defence University, Islamabad, Pakistan.)

4 National Security Policy of Pakistan 2022-2026, p. 34.

5 Stephen P. Cohen, *The Idea of Pakistan* (Washington, D.C.: Brookings Institution Press, 2004), p. 270.

6 https://www.ndtv.com/world-news/pahalgam-terror-attack-comes-days-after-pakistan-army-chiefs-jugular-vein-remark-on-kashmir-8233159 accessed on 27 Apr 25.

7 https://southasianvoices.org/pakistan-full-spectrum-deterrence-trends-trajectories/ accessed on 23 Apr 25.

8 http://eng.chinamil.com.cn/CHINA_209163/MOOTW/CounterTerrorism/News_209173/16368509.html accessed on 24 Apr 25.

9 https://thediplomat.com/2024/01/the-importance-of-china-and-pakistans-joint-naval-exercises/ accessed on 23 Apr 25.

10 https://www.eurasiantimes.com/after-pakistan-air-force-chinas-plaaf-is-now-exercising-with-more-air-forces-to-sharpen-its-combat-edge/ accessed on 24 Apr 25.

11 https://www.civitas.org.uk/content/files/China-training.pdf accessed on 23 Apr 25.

12 https://www.civitas.org.uk/publications/inadvertently-arming-china-one-year-on/ accessed on 25 Apr 25.

13 http://www.chinadaily.com.cn/china/2011-03/20/content_12199043.htm accessed on 25 Apr 25.

14 https://africacenter.org/spotlight/china-united-front-africa/ accessed on 23 Apr 25.

15 https://africacenter.org/spotlight/china-pla-military-political-work-pme-africa/ accessed on 25 Apr 25.

16 Mark Mazzetti, Helene Cooper, and Peter Baker, "Behind the Hunt for Bin Laden," *New York Times*, May 2, 2011, https://www.nytimes.com/2011/05/03/world/asia/03intel.html; and "Pakistan Outrage after 'Nato Attack Kills Soldiers'," BBC, November 26, 2011, https://www.bbc.com/news/world-asia-15901363.

17 Paul J. Smith, "The China–Pakistan–United States Strategic Triangle: From Cold War to the 'War on Terrorism,'" *Asian Affairs: An American Review*, Vol. 38, No. 4 (2011), pp. 197–220.

18 Missy Ryan, "Key Nations Sit Out U.S. Standoff with Russia, China, Leaks Show," *Washington Post*, April 29, 2023, https://www.washingtonpost.com/national-security/2023/04/29/biden-foreign-policy-discord-leaks/.

19 Ibid.

20 Anwar Iqbal, "Pakistan Walking Diplomatic Tightrope Between US, Rivals," *Dawn*, 01 May2023, https://www.dawn.com/news/1750266/pakistan-walking-diplomatic-tightrope-between-us-rivals.

21 https://www.scmp.com/news/china/military/article/3302515/china-supplied-81-pakistans-arms-imports-past-5-years-sipri-says accessed on 24 Apr 25.

22 Daniel Markey, *China's Western Horizon: Beijing and the New Geopolitics of Eurasia* (New York: Oxford University Press, 2020).

23 https://www.hudson.org/national-security-defense/the-ideologies-of-south-asian-jihadi-groups#:~:text=The%20president%20of%20the%20ruling,%2C%20to%20 promote%20Pan%2DIslamism accessed on 25 Feb 25.

24 https://swarajyamag.com/world/rogue-maybe-but-the-one-thing-pakistan-is-not-is-a-failed-state accessed on 24 Feb 25.

25 https://carnegieendowment.org/research/2016/04/pakistan-at-the-crossroads?lang=en accessed on 24 Feb 25.

26 https://comparative-politics-and-international-studies-series-jaffrelot-christophe-lour-laurence-pan-islamic-connections-transnational-networks-between-south-asia-and-the-gulf-oxford-university-pre-pdf-free.html accessed on 24 Feb 25.

27 Ahmed, Z. S., & Karim, U. (2024). Saudi Arabia's soft power in Pakistan. *Journal of Political Power*, *17*(1), 42–64. https://doi.org/10.1080/2158379X.2024.2341024 accessed on 21 Feb 25.

28 https://tribune.com.pk/story/2527699/saudi-arabia-leads-pakistans-remittance-growth-with-252-increase-in-jan# accessed on 23 Feb 25.

29 Ahmed, Z. S., & Karim, U. (2024). Saudi Arabia's soft power in Pakistan. *Journal of Political Power*, *17*(1), 42–64. https://doi.org/10.1080/2158379X.2024.2341024 accessed on 21 Feb 25.

30 N Naviwala, 04 September 2015. Playing Hardball with Aid to Pakistan. Foreign Policy. http://foreignpolicy.com/2015/09/04/playing-hardball-with-aid-to-pakistan/(open in a new window) accessed on 21 Feb 25.

31 Karim, U., 2023b. Pakistan and Saudi Ties: an overview of political, strategic, economic and defence linkages. In: U. Karim and S. Kapur, eds. *Regional Security in South Asia and the Gulf*. New York: Routledge, 152–179.

32 Shabbir, S, 05 August 2022b. Saudi KS Relief hands over second emergency relief consignment for Pakistani flood victims. https://www.arabnews.pk/node/2136606/pakistan a new window.

33 Fatima Zahid Ali, Kevin Smets & Benjamin De Cleen. (2024) Pakistani transgender activists on Instagram: The politics of postcolonial language appropriation and abrogation. *International Journal of Media & Cultural Politics* 20:1, pp. 91-113.

34 Waterman, D., 2014. Saudi Wahhabi Imperialism in Pakistan: history, legacy, contemporary representations and debates. Societal Studies, 6 (2), 242–258. doi:10.13165/SMS-14-6-2-02.

35 Zweiri, M., & James, T.B. (2021). Saudi Arabia–Pakistan Relations: An Age of Uncertainty or Decline? Contemporary Review of the Middle East, 8(4), 496-511. https://doi.org/10.1177/23477989211031793.

36 TL Friedman, 13 November 2001. In Pakistan, it's Jihad 101. *The New York Times*. https://www.nytimes.com/2001/11/13/opinion/foreign-affairs-in-pakistan-it-s-jihad-101.html accessed on 24 Apr 23.

37 T Rahman, 2000. The teaching of Arabic to the Muslims of South Asia. Islamic Studies, pp. 399–443.

38 A Shah, 04 Jan 19. Saudi Arabia offers 583 scholarships to Pakistani students. *Arab News*. https://www.arabnews.pk/node/1430316/pakistan accessed on 19 Sep 2021.

39 https://espace.library.uq.edu.au/data/UQ_238095/IslamicStudies and IslamicEducation.pdf accessed on 26 Oct 24.

40 Pandith, F., 24 March 2019. Extremism is Riyadh's top export. *Foreign Policy*. https://foreignpolicy.com/2019/03/24/farah-pandith-saudi-how-we-win-book.

41 Sib Kaifee, Saudi-Pak Ties: "One of the closest relationships in the world", June 13, 2020, *Arab News*, https://www.arabnews.pk/node/1453546/pakistan

42 Adeela Naureen, Waqar K Kauravi, The deep-rooted ties with Saudi Arabia, *The Express Tribune*, January 17, 2022. httos://tribune.com.ok/storv/2396198/the-deep-rooted-ties-with-saudi-arabia

43 Safdar Sial, Emerging Dynamics in Pakistan Saudi Relations, Norwegian Peacebuilding Centre, https://www.files.ethz.ch/isn/195227/202d14d49238cab72b99e625383101d3.pdf

44 https://www.voanews.com/a/ex-pakistan-army-chief-to-lead-anti-terrorism-coalition/3667870.html accessed on 11 May 25.

45 Soharwardy Syed B, Wahabization-Salafization of Pakistan and Muslim Ummah,Fighting the Terrorists But Supporting Their Ideology. https://www.islamicsupremecouncil.com/wahabization-salafization-of-muslims/ accessed on 14 Apr 24.

46 Abdul Shaban, (2015). "Urdu and Urdu Medium Schools in Maharashtra." Economic and Political Weekly. 50(29), pp. 46-51.

47 S Mir Khetran, (2016). "Economic Connectivity: Pakistan, China, West Asia and Central Asia." *Strategic Studies*. 36(4), pp. 61-76.

48 Ihsan Yilmaz, (2021). *Creating the Desired Citizens: State, Islam and Ideology in Turkey*. Cambridge and New York: Cambridge University Press, 2021.

49 B Avari, (2016). *Islamic Civilization in South Asia: A History of Muslim Power and Presence*. Routledge: New York, accessed on 07 Mar 25.

50 C Mudde, (2004). "The Populist Zeitgeist." *Government and Opposition*. 39, pp. 541–563.

51 https://foreignpolicy.com/2020/09/05/ertugrul-turkey-dizi-soft-power-pakistan/ accessed on 07 Mar 25.

52 P Taguieff, (1995). "Political Science Confronts Populism: From a Conceptual Mirage to a Real Problem." *Telos*. 103, pp. 9–43.

53 https://tribune.com.pk/article/97102/why-is-pakistan-the-only-country-that-does-not-recognise-armenia accessed on 07 Mar 25.

54 https://www.trtworld.com/art-culture/tv-series-to-show-asian-muslims-role-in-turkish-war-of-independence-43125 accessed on 07 Mar 25.

55 Mushtaq, Nadia. (2004). "Pak-Turkey Relations: Towards Cooperative Future." *Strategic Studies.* 24(2), pp. 89-116.

56 Ihsan Yilmaz,(2021). *Creating the Desired Citizens: State, Islam and Ideology in Turkey.* Cambridge and New York: Cambridge University Press, 2021.

57 https://www.jpost.com/middle-east/turkey-pakistan-malaysia-and-qatar-form-troubling-new-alliance-629519 accessed on 07 Mar 25.

58 https://sundayguardianlive.com/world/pak-emerges-as-major-supplier-of-ammunition-to-ukraine-in-war-with-russia accessed on 03 Aug 23.

59 National Security Policy of Pakistan 2022-2026, p. 24.

60 https://www.ptinews.com/story/international/pakistan-to-launch-new-operation-against-terrorism/1603106 accessed on 23 Apr 25

61 The Constitution of Islamic Republic of Pakistan 1973. https://na.gov.pk/documents accessed on 03 Aug 23.

62 Defence Policy of Pakistan 2022-26, p. 41.

63 RAND Corp, "Mil Doctrine", https://www.rand.org/topics/militarydoctrine.html accessed on 12 Jul 23.

64 Brig S.K. Malik, *The Quranic Concept of War* (Lahore, Pakistan: Associated Printers, 1979), p. 01.

65 Pakistan Army's motto used to be 'Ittehad, Yaqeen aur Tanzeem' (Unity, Faith and Discipline), insisting on functional attributes that reside in any militaristic framework. The motto of the Pakistani Army was changed to a decidedly religious 'Imaan, Taqwa, Jihad fi Sabilillah' (Faith, Piety, Holy War in the path of Allah).

66 Ibid, p. 23.

67 Lieutenant General Ghulam Muhammad Malik, 'Islamic Concept of Leadership' in *Pakistan Army Green Book* (Lahore: Feroz Sons Pvt. Ltd., 1990), p. 13.

68 https://www.ebsco.com/research-starters/politics-and-government/directorate-inter-services-intelligence-isi accessed on 24 Apr 25.

69 Manpreet Sethi, Pakistan's Nuclear Doctrine and Strategy, *Air Power Journal,* Vol. 2, No. 3 Monsoon, 2007 (Jul-Sep), pp. 02-03.

70 Sehrish Naz Fellow of Sociology, University of Sargodha, Pakistan's Military Strategy: Challenges and Response. Electronic Research Journal of Social Sciences and Humanities Vol. 1, Issue I, Jan-Mar 2019 www.eresearchjournal.com.

71 Nazariya-e-Pakistan – https://www.dawn.com/2012/08/13/nazariya-e-pakistan/? Accessed on 03 Aug 23. Dr Moeen Aldeen Aqeel, Nazariya-e-Pakistan aur Quaid-e-Azam, Bookhome, Jan 2020.

72 https://time.com/7284470/india-pakistan-water-supply-climate-change/ accessed on 10 May 25.

73 Uzair Younus, "Geopolitics and the IMF: Delusion or Myopia?," Dawn, 21 June 23 accessed on 23 Apr 25. https://www.dawn.com/news/1760961/geopolitics-and-the-imf-delusion-or-myopia.

74 SDG-6: Country Acceleration Case Study: Pakistan, UNOhttps://www.unwater.org/sites/default/files/2022-09/CountryAccelerationCaseStudies_2022_Pakistan_ENGLISH.pdf accessed on 21 Apr 25.

75 https://www.atlanticcouncil.org/in-depth-research-reports/issue-brief/rescuing-pakistans-economy/ accessed on 21 Apr 25.

76 https://earthjournalism.net/stories/world-bank-drainage-project-leads-to-loss-of-livelihoods-in-pakistan accessed on 22 Apr 25.

77 https://www.dawn.com/news/1381735#:~:text=More%20than%20two%2Dthirds%20of,dysentery%20and%20hepatitis%20are%20rampant accessed on 23 Apr 25.

78 Country's water storage capacity on the decline- https://www.dawn.com/news/1607566?ref accessed on 25 Jul 23.

79 https://www.ilo.org/sites/default/files/wcmsp5/groups/public/@asia/@ro-bangkok/@ilo-islamabad/documents/publication/wcms_554877.pdf accessed on 11 May 25.

80 Pakistan Migration Snapshot, Aug 2019, International Org for Migration (IOM), UN Migration Agency, p. 32.

81 https://pakistan.unfpa.org/sites/default/files/pub-pdf/pakistan_psa_2020_final_report.pdf accessed on 11 May 25.

82 https://timesofindia.indiatimes.com/blogs/no-free-lunch/the-curious-partnership-between-communist-china-and-the-islamic-state-of-pakistan/ accessed on 25 Apr 25.

Six

Modus Vivendi for the Future

Introduction

India-Pakistan relations have remained in a state of stasis for the last five years since the revocation of Article 370, with Pakistan suspending trade and downgrading diplomatic relations with India.[1] The calcification of stands by both countries notwithstanding, the CFU[2] between both the nations along the LoC has held as Pakistan has a restive western border to deal with and India is handling the aggression of the PLA on its northern borders. Any forward movement would be highly dependent on either of the nations softening their hardened stance, with India maintaining a '*no talks with terror*'[3] position while Pakistan wants India to '*undo the revocation of Article 370*'.[4] The elections in Pakistan have raised a sliver of hope for rapprochement with Pakistan's political dispensation looking for a way out of the present logjam. Mr. Nawaz Sharif, on assuming the leadership of his party in May 2024 had said, "*On May 28, 1998, Pakistan carried out five nuclear tests. After that Vajpayee Saheb came here and made an agreement with us. But we violated that agreement; it was our fault.*"[5]

Perennial Challenges

Cultural Divergence. The inability to find common ground for a robust and meaningful dialogue has marred the trajectory of India-Pakistan relations. The cultural divergence steeped in the mistrust and agony of Partition has framed the strategic culture of the Pakistan military. The success of the 'Two Nation Theory' propounded by the founders of Pakistan lies in the idea of communal disharmony of India, wherein the people of two religions were not meant to coexist. The survey conducted as part of research for this thesis was unequivocal in the opinion that the Pakistan military's strategic culture is predicated on enmity with India on the unfinished business of Partition, be it the division of assets or the territory of Jammu and Kashmir. Nearly 204 of the 262 respondents believe that anti-India sentiment drives the strategic culture of the Pakistan military creating the revisionist mindset (Fig. 25). This mindset has ensured that even when the political dispensation has attempted to bridge the gap, the military has scuttled the plan.

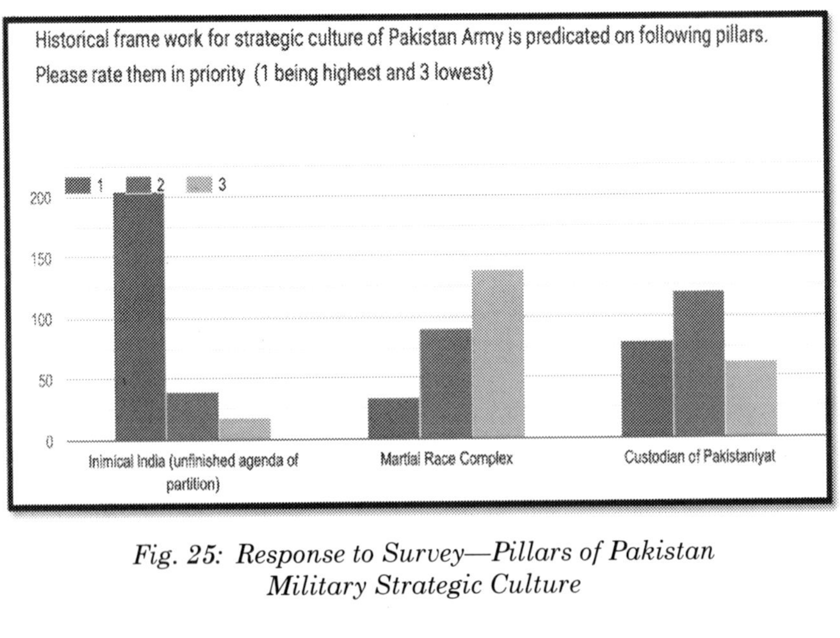

Fig. 25: Response to Survey—Pillars of Pakistan Military Strategic Culture

Decision-Making Hierarchy. The decision-making hierarchy in both nations is misaligned to dialogue; the same was commented upon in the book, '*Not War Not Peace*' by Toby Dalton and George Perkowhich published in 2016.[6] A diagrammatic representation of their argument (Fig. 26) indicates the dissonance. In the hierarchy illustrated below, the Indian political dispensation cannot be seen speaking to the Pakistan military and when the Pakistan politicians try and speak to Indian politicians, the Pakistan military steps in as it considers itself to be the final arbitrator on all matters concerning India and cannot let go of the power it wields. Indian diplomats fail to cut any ice with the Pakistan military as they are not used to military methods and processes and the dialogue again fails. This dissonance in decision making does not allow the Indian military to establish links with the Pakistan military as the bureaucrats and politicians cannot allow it to happen. Hence, a permanent state of limbo persists. Attempts to break this logjam have proved unsuccessful. The Lahore Declaration[7] that was scuttled by the Pakistan Army and the Agra Summit[8] proved to be inconclusive and the initial peace overtures by PM Narendra Modi were scuttled by terrorist attacks in Pathankot and Uri.[9]

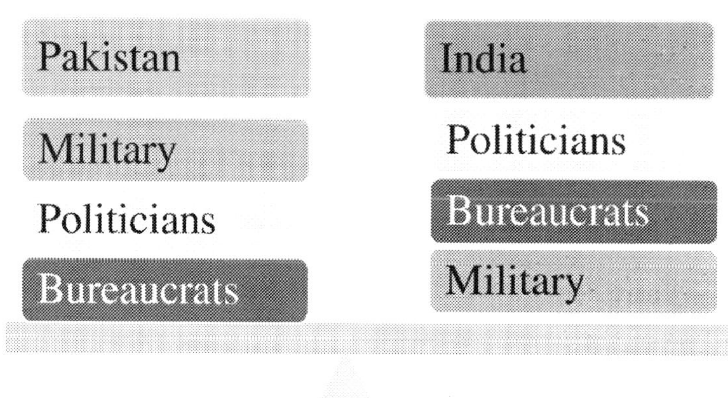

Fig. 26: Decision Making Hierarchy

Fig. 27: Survey Results—Pakistan Military

Terrorist Assembly Line. The terrorist assembly line functional in Pakistan demands an outlet; in case they are denied an outlet towards India, the likelihood is that they would join terrorist groups that are seeking leverage within Pakistan and exacerbate the challenges being faced by the Pakistan security apparatus on their western borders and for internal security, the two dimensions of the proverbial '*triple stretch*' (Fig. 26).[10] The recruitment base of anti-India terrorist groups is primarily Punjab and Sindh but in case they are not provided with a target to wage jihad against, they could turn on the other sects in Pakistan and also target security forces that may be branded as 'kafir' by some religious leaders for having launched operations against 'mujahideen'.[11] One of the survey questions produced responses (Fig. 27) indicative of an exacerbated intra-sect rift within Sunni Islam in Pakistan. The Pakistan military has no other option but to keep the anti-India agenda and freedom of Kashmir alive to ensure their own internal safety and security. The terrorist groups once under the total control of the Pakistan military may have broken free from their shackles and may operate on their own accord as well.[12]

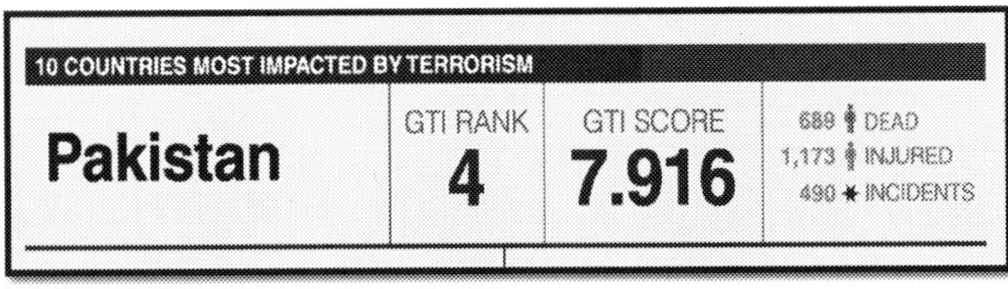

Fig. 28: Global Terrorism Index-2023[13]

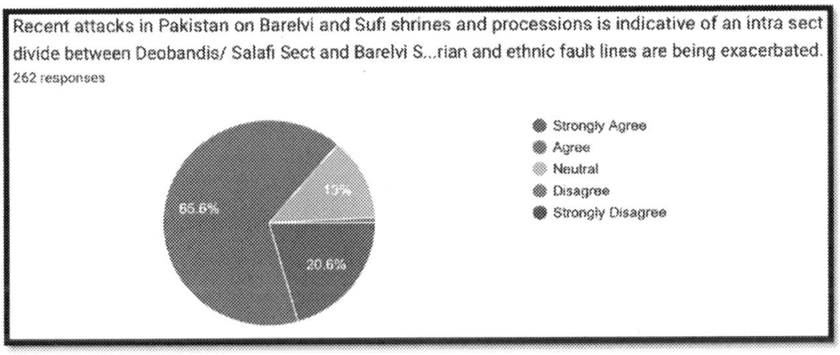

Fig. 29: Response to Survey on Intra-sect Fault Lines

Rentier State to China. Pakistan has been pedalling its geo-strategic location and assets to the highest bidder. The rentier state status with respect to China is now complete after the withdrawal of US forces from Afghanistan. The control of China on the Pakistani economy through the CPEC and the Pakistan military by funding and equipment provision has forced Pakistan to take decisions which are only driven by Chinese interests (Figs. 28 & 29).[14] Hussain Haqqani, a former diplomat of Pakistan, says, "*Ironically, CPEC is seen by Pakistan not merely in economic terms but as a security guarantee of China's commitment to their country.*"[15] The stakes of China in Pakistan are so large that Pakistan has no option but to respond to the machinations of China. The ongoing tension between China and India offers China an avenue to keep India engaged on the western borders thereby exacerbating the resource availability of the Indian armed forces, creating a two-front scenario. The future trajectory of India-Pakistan interaction will ipso-facto be dictated by China.

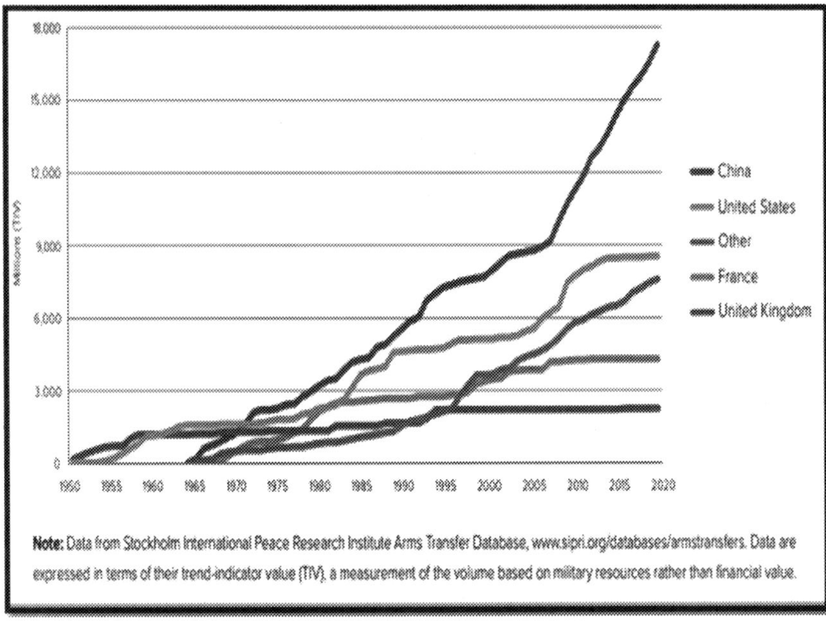

Fig. 30: Cumulative Defence Exports to Pakistan[16]

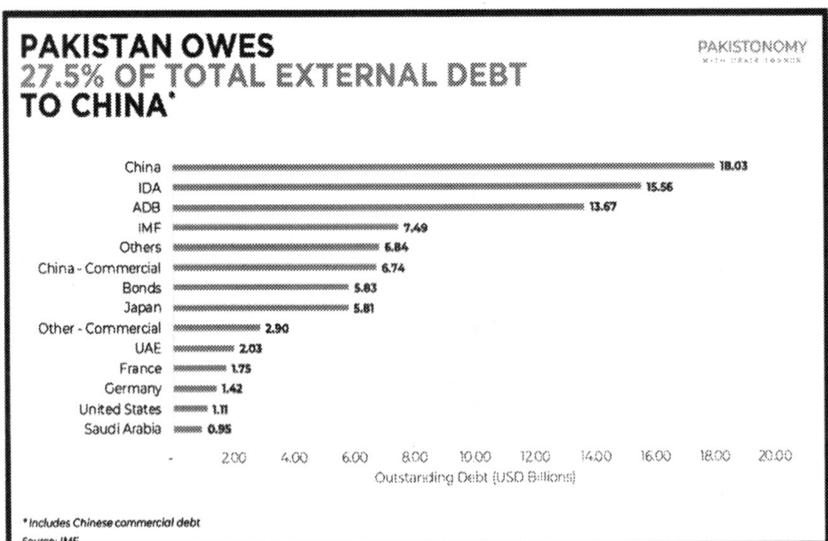

Fig. 31: Debt Exposure to China-Pakistan at Pole Position

Policy Options for India

The challenges listed above are constant. The leverages that exist with India to alter the behavioural pattern exist in three domains—geo-economics, diplomacy and military. The options available to India are elaborated in the succeeding paragraphs.

Indian Geo-economics Policy: Olive Branch

The etymology of 'geo-economics' dates back to 1990 and is credited to American author, Edward Luttwak. In an article written prior to the disintegration of the Soviet Union, Luttwak presented the term as an 'admixture of the logic of conflict with the methods of commerce.'[17] Geo-economics measures national power against matrices of economic indicators and Pakistan fares poorly on all markers. The country's external debt and liabilities is USD 124.3 billion as in June 2023[18] and is ranked 161 out of 192 countries on the Human Development Index.[19] The gauntlet of revival of the Pakistan economy has been picked up by the Pakistan military to resurrect it, both for its organizational interests and for redeeming its image in the polity of nations. This offers a key leverage to India. Prior to suspension of trade in 2019, Pakistan's imports annually from India was approximately USD 2 billion, and exports were nearly USD 500 million.[20] The geo-economic framework aims to exploit Pakistan's geography by focusing on connectivity and development of partnerships/alignments with the world. The Pakistan Army has a vision as part of the Munir doctrine to act as the trade, transit, and production hub by connecting West, Central, and South Asia and gradually move away from primarily assistance-based relationships to prioritizing trade and investment relationships with countries across geopolitical fault lines. This strategic approach is centred on maximizing Pakistan's economic gains to avoid subservience to major powers and increase its room for manoeuvre.[21]

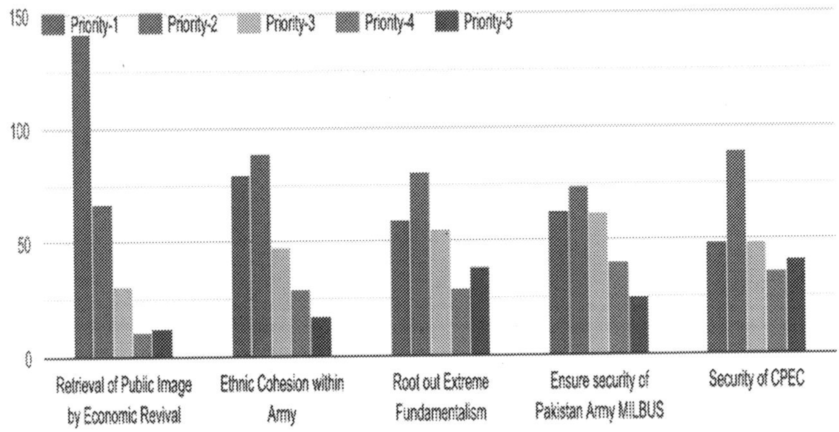

Fig. 32: Priority for General Asim Munir

Normalized economic relations could create conditions for India and Pakistan to consolidate economic gains.[22] It would unlock the potential of the East-West axis in South Asia, leading to enhanced regional networks that operate omni-directionally. Mutual access to land routes would improve trade relations between the two countries and make the whole region more connected. Through overland routes, India and Pakistan will be able to connect with markets in Central Asia and East Asia. Both regions are very important for the two countries; gaining access to East Asian markets will help Pakistan diversify its exports and actualize its 'Vision East Asia Policy'. As for India, it needs to make greater inroads into Central Asia to get access to energy resources (TAPI being a case in point).[23] Trade in South Asia has the capacity to rise from USD 23 billion to USD 67 billion if trade barriers are removed.[24] World Bank estimates envisage the trade potential between India and Pakistan on an annual basis to be USD 37 billion, compared to the existing volume of USD 2 Billion.[25] As per a World Bank report, "*85 per cent of the unrealized regional potential trade for Pakistan is with India.*"[26]

If India is to create leverage with the Pakistan military it would be prudent to assist Pakistan revive its economy, thus providing a fillip to the Pakistan military's standing within the nation and also ensure that geo-economics drives the geo-politics between the two states. The survey conducted for this book also points to the fact that restoration of the Pakistan Military's image through economic revival and protection of Pakistan's MILBUS are key to the success of the Munir doctrine. Of the 262 responses, 53 per cent considered restoration of the Pakistan military's reputation by economic revival as priority-1 for General Munir (Fig. 30). Pakistan's new political dispensation too has indicated a desire to reopen trade with India,[27] an aspiration, if pursued, would mark a major diplomatic shift and indicate the Pakistan military's willingness to engage with India.

Indian Diplomatic Policy: Triple Pincer

A Pakistan that is politically and economically stable, and which does not use jihad as a lever of foreign policy, would be an ideal end-state for India. However, this would demand a review of Pakistan's view of India as an existential threat; stop seeking strategic depth in Afghanistan, stop offering the geography of Pakistan on rent to the great powers, and curb exploitation of Islamist groups as useful instruments to advance domestic and regional policies. The ability of Indian diplomatic manoeuvres to achieve the stated end-state would be based on three pillars; one, the heft India has with Middle Eastern states like Saudi Arabia, the UAE and Qatar; two, the USA to re-integrate with Pakistan to ensure there are leverages available in Washington; and lastly, a closer relation of India with Afghanistan.[28]

A combination of persuasion, dissuasion and coercion using the three pillars may yield positive results as the Pakistan military would prefer to stabilize the internal security situation and make Pakistan look a more lucrative destination for economic activity. FDI from the Middle East is being considered the panacea to Pakistan's economic woes[29] and if geo-politics is integrated with geo-economics, Pakistan may be forced to alter its trajectory. The heft India has developed in the Middle East and the GCC has the capacity to influence their funding to Pakistan.[30] The tenet of the Munir doctrine to develop a closer relationship with the USA[31] offers India leverage based on the strategic partnership of the USA and India. The engagement of India with the Taliban at various levels had commenced with an Indian delegation participating in the Regional Cooperation Initiative meeting in Kabul under the leadership of the Taliban on 29 January 2024.[32] Furthermore, on 7 March 2024, an Indian delegation led by Joint Secretary J.P. Singh of the Ministry of External Affairs had an exhaustive interaction with Taliban Foreign Minister Muttaqi on expansion of bilateral ties, especially on economic and transit matters.[33] The growing proximity of India with Taliban-led Afghanistan has created a fair degree of alarm in Pakistan and would be a key leverage to coerce and dissuade Pakistan from engaging on a path of belligerence and force the Pakistan military to recalibrate its response as their relationship with the Taliban continues to deteriorate.[34]

Indian Military Policy: Pay Back in a Grey Zone

Grey zone aggression is an intricate campaign to attain political objectives while operating below the threshold of a full-blown war. Such campaigns involve an incremental application of vectors of CNP to achieve desired results without triggering a decisive military response[35] (Fig. 33). India has been at the receiving end of Pakistan's grey zone warfare since 1947 and has been reticent in responding in the same domain. Each act of belligerence by Pakistan in the grey zone has been responded to by India in the conventional domain (Fig. 34) less the actions after 2016 where in the use of conventional vectors have been used against sub-conventional targets.

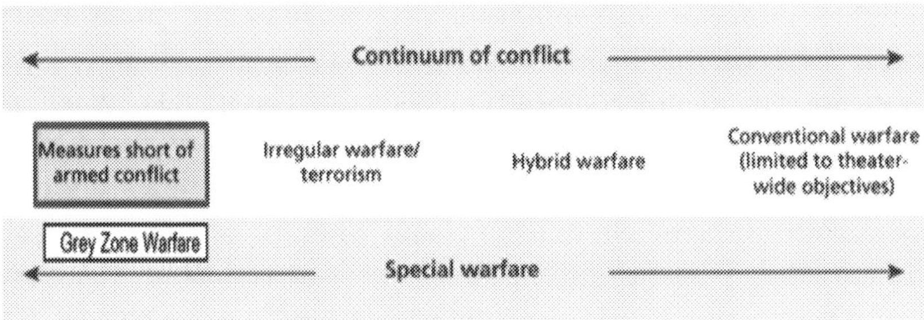

Fig. 33: Typology of Conflict[36]

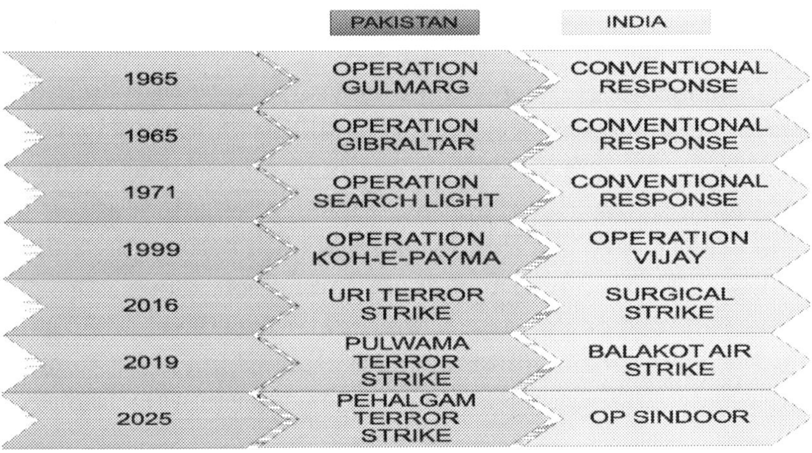

Fig. 34: Response Matrix of India-Pakistan Conflict

The Indian armed forces' capabilities to pay back in the same coin in the grey zone would force the Pakistan military to look at its options against India afresh and impose necessary caution on them in the spectrum of conflict. The development of multi-domain capacity to operate in the grey zone is not only a matter of employing existing capabilities in a focused way but developing niche competencies. Not all grey zone challenges can be viewed as implied tasks of major combat operations. The requirement for operations in the grey zone demands some degree of priority emphasis, in capability development, force design, posture and technology investments. The armed forces are rightly focused on being ready for major combat operations; however, on a day-to-day basis, the capabilities that will be in the highest demand are those for the ongoing competition below the threshold of war.[37] It is thus necessary to balance between emphasis on inter-state regular conflict and grey zone capabilities learning a lesson from the recent conflcits where drones and Unmanned Systems in all dimensions air, land and sea have proven to be the choice of weapon in order to reduce human costs of war on the nation prosecuting them. In an era of rising inter-state interactions in the C5 continuum, India's adversaries are increasingly looking to campaigns of grey zone actions to achieve an overwhelming advantage. The Indian armed forces, to succeed in this realm, will have to take grey zone aggression seriously as a distinct area of strategy and create concepts, capabilities and technologies for the purpose of deterrence by denial and punishment unique to this domain of warfare. Russian President Vladimir Putin has stated that the nation that leads in AI "will become the ruler of the world."[38] The advancement of AI in present day warfare will forever alter the balance of power at strategic level and combat ratios in tactical domain. For this reason, China has committed 150 billion dollars to become the world leader in AI technology.[39]

In four years of conflict in Syria from 2014 to 2018, the United Kingdom used Reaper drones more than 2,400 times during strategic missions, the equivalent of two per day. The Pentagon estimates that by 2035, remotely piloted aircraft will make up 70 percent of the U.S. Air Force.[40] Meanwhile, Israel has been developing its own weaponized drones, and it has deployed drones in Gaza to conduct surveillance, deliver explosives, and more. Furthermore, drone technology is spreading rapidly to militaries around the world. Nearly every NATO member state now has the capability to use drones in conflict. Closer home both China and Pakistan. In the last five years, have also created drone manufacturing programs. China currently supplies Pakistan with its Wing Loong and CH-series drones, while Turkey has established a production facility of TB-2 drones in Pakistan.[41] Even non-state actors are using drones. Hezbollah has used

Iranian-built reconnaissance drones to violate Israeli airspace, while Hamas has been using drones against Israel since October 2023. AI in concert with drones in warfare is spreading rapidly. Israel has also used the "Lavender" AI system in the conflict in Gaza to identify 37,000 Hamas targets.[42] Accordingly, the current conflict between Israel and Hamas has been dubbed the first "AI war"[43] which is exploitation of disruptive technology in non-contact but kinetic vectors of warfare a key determinant of Grey Zone warfare.

Conclusion

It is time the Pakistan military moves past a debate about whether to own the (mis)conception of its strategic culture that is wedded to a revisionist mindset with respect to India or take to cooperation rather than competition with India. If Pakistan is serious about achieving positive comprehensive national security outcomes and the Munir doctrine aspirations have to be brought to fruition, it has to shed its anti-India rhetoric. The real challenge is how and at what pace can this idea be mainstreamed and who will do it. Does the present combine of Munir along with the Sharif family complete the geo-economic pivot that offers Pakistan the best chance to achieve the 'safety, security, dignity, and prosperity' of its citizens while ensuring its traditional security needs are adequately met. It is also prudent for the Indian dispensation to calibrate a multi-pronged approach of *Olive Branch, Triple Pincer* and *Payback* to leverage the Pakistan military establishment's sensitivity to economic development and use the present political dispensation in Pakistan to seek better conditions in the subcontinent to achieve its desired vision of *Viksit Bharat@2047*. The India-Pakistan relation in the present domain is stuck in limbo between the Cooperation and Conflict paradigm of the C5 Continuum and in case no forward movement is possible, the nuclear armed neighbours are going to be entwined in grey zone contestation for time immemorial with both cooperation and conflict ruled out. (Fig. 35).

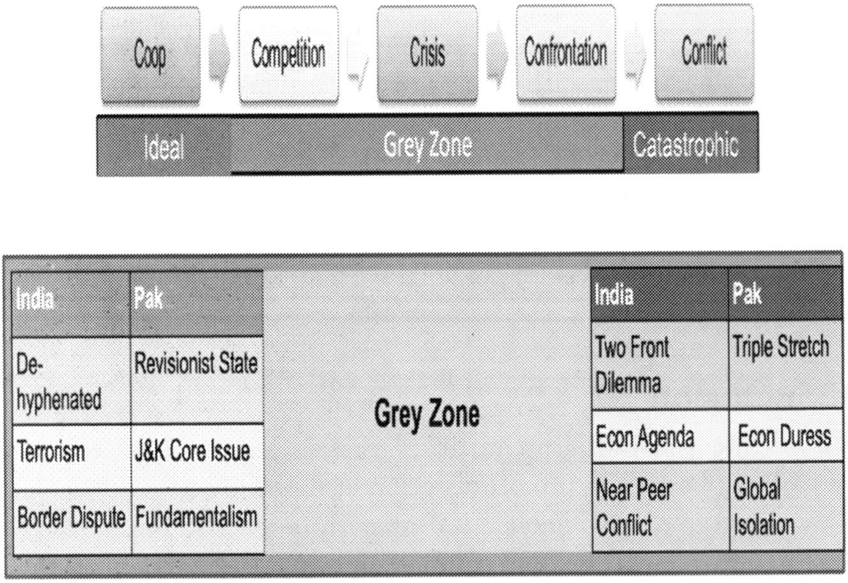

Fig. 35: India-Pakistan Paradox

NOTES

1 https://edition.cnn.com/2019/08/07/asia/kashmir-pakistan-response-intl-hnk/index.html accessed on 23 Jun 24.

2 https://www.thehindu.com/news/national/india-pakistan-agree-to-ceasefire-along-border/article61746932.ece accessed on 21 Jun 24.

3 https://www.orfonline.org/expert-speak/if-talks-and-terror-cant-go-together-neither-can-trade-and-terror accessed on 21 Jun 24.

4 https://www.livemint.com/news/world/pakistan-says-will-challenge-revoking-of-article-370-1564996777281.html accessed on 21 Jun 24.

5 https://www.hindustantimes.com/india-news/india-responds-to-nawaz-sharif-s-remarks-calls-it-a-perspective-based-on-reality-101717085193156.html#:~:text=Following%20his%20re%2Delection%20as,Sharif%20said%2C%20speaking %20 in%20Urdu.accessed on 21 Jun 24.

6 Perkovich George and Toby Dalton, Not War, Not Peace? Motivating Pakistan to Prevent Cross-Border Terrorism, New Delhi: Oxford University Press, 2016, p. 27.

7 https://www.belfercenter.org/publication/diplomatic-fiasco-pakistans-failure-diplomatic-front-nullifies-its-gains-battlefield accessed on 25 Jun 24.

8 https://economictimes.indiatimes.com/news/politics-and-nation/musharrafs-comment-on-failed-agra-summit-hidden-hand-says-maine-dekha-hai/articleshow/7060297.cms?from=mdr accessed on 21 Jun 24.

9 https://www.stimson.org/wp-content/files/file-attachments/InvestigatingCrises.pdf accessed on 21 Jun 24.
10 https://www.dawn.com/news/783306/pakistans-triple-front accessed on 12 May 24.
11 https://www.idsa.in/system/files/book/tehrik-e-taliban-pakistan-book.pdf accessed on 12 May 24.
12 https://www.state.gov/reports/country-reports-on-terrorism-2022/pakistan/ accessed on 13 May 24.
13 https://www.economicsandpeace.org/wp-content/uploads/2024/02/GTI-2024-web-290224.pdf accessed on 01 Jul 24.
14 Fair, C. Christine, et al. "Pakistan's Army: Running and Ruining a Country." *Asia Policy*, no. 19, 2015, pp. 163–67. *JSTOR*, http://www.jstor.org/stable/24905309. Accessed 30 June 2024.
15 https://www.orfonline.org/research/pakistan-staring-at-scary-future accessed on 23 Jun 24.
16 https://www.orfonline.org/expert-speak/analysing-trends-arms-transfer-china-pakistan accessed on 23 Jun24.
17 LuttwakEdward N., "From Geopolitics to Geo-Economics: Logic of Conflict, Grammar of Commerce," The National Interest, no. 20 (1990): 17–23.
18 State Bank of Pakistan.https://www.sbp.org.pk/ecodata/index2.asp.
19 Report 2021/2022 - Human Development Reports, https://hdr.undp.org/system/files/ documents/global-report-document/hdr2021-22pdf_1.pdf.
20 https://www.csmonitor.com/World/Asia-South-Central/2024/0401/Suspending-trade-with-India-has-cost-Pakistan.-Can-the-new-government-shift-gears accessed on 01 Jul 24.
21 https://www.mei.edu/publications/pakistans-military-and-foreign-policy-under-gen-asim-munir accessed on 01 Jul 24.
22 Constantino Xavier, "Sambandh as Strategy: India's New Approach to Regional Connectivity," Brookings India,https://www.brookings.edu/wp-content/uploads/2020/01/Sambandh-as-Strategy-Indias-regional-connectivity-initiative.pdf/ accessed on 01 Jul 24.
23 "Peace with Pakistan will give India direct access to Central Asia: PM Khan," Business Standard, March 17, 2021, https://www.business-standard.com/article/ international/peace-with-pakistan-will-give-india-direct-access-to-central-asia-pm- khan-121031700738_1.html/. accessed on 01 Jul 24.
24 World Bank Group, "Pakistan's Trade with South Asia Can Rise by Eight-Fold – A New World Bank Report," World Bank, December 5, 2018, https://www.worldbank.org/en/news/press-release/2018/12/05/pakistan-could-boost-trade-with-south-asia-eight-fold/.
25 Ibid.
26 World Bank Group, "Pakistan@100 Regional Connectivity," World Bank, March 2019, https://openknowledge.worldbank.org/server/api/core/bitstreams/ddb936ac-9cb0-57a9-b7076928125662df/content/ accessed on 01 Jul 24.
27 https://www.csmonitor.com/World/Asia-South-Central/2024/0401/Suspending-trade-with-India-has-cost-Pakistan.-Can-the-new-government-

shift-gears accessed on 01 Jul 24.

28 https://www.thehindu.com/news/national/india-engaging-the-taliban-in-various-formats-says-mea-spokesperson/article67801854.ece accessed on 01 Jul 24.

29 https://thefridaytimes.com/04-Sep-2023/the-munir-doctrine-blast-bulldoze-disregard-all-obstacles-to-economic-recovery accessed on 01 Jul 24.

30 https://sundayguardianlive.com/opinion/india-and-middle-east-seeking-an-alignment-in-bilateral-interests accessed on 02 Jul 24.

31 https://tribune.com.pk/story/2427668/coas-centcom-chief-discuss-regional-security accessed on 01 Jul 24.

32 https://www.icwa.in/show_content.php?lang=1&level=3&ls_id=10459& lid=6670 accessed on 02 Jul 24.

33 https://thediplomat.com/2024/03/where-do-taliban-pakistan-relations-stand-now/ accessed on 02 Jul 24.

34 https://www.aljazeera.com/news/2023/8/17/talibans-ties-with-pakistan-fraying-amid-mounting-security-concerns accessed on 02 Jul 24.

35 Some of the official and unofficial statements on gray zone activities in the past few years include International Security Advisory Board, Report on Gray Zone Conflict, Washington, D.C.: U.S. Department of State, 03 Jan 2017; Nathan P. Freier, Outplayed: Regaining Initiative in the Gray Zone, Carlisle, US Army War College, Strategic Studies Institute, Jun 2016; and Michael J. Mazarr, Mastering the Gray Zone, Carlisle, US Army War College, Strategic Studies Institute, Dec 2015.

36 Hoffman Frank G., "Examining Complex Forms of Conflict: Gray Zone and Hybrid Challenges," Prism, Vol. 7, No. 4, November 2018, p. 31.

37 Bratton, P.C. (2020). The Not So GrayZone in South Asia. Comparative Strategy, 39(1), 41–61. https://doi.org/10.1080/01495933.2020.1702346.

38 https://www.theverge.com/2017/9/4/16251226/russia-ai-putin-rule-the-world accessed on 01 May 25.

39 Roberts, H., Cowls, J., Morley, J. *et al.* The Chinese approach to artificial intelligence: an analysis of policy, ethics, and regulation. *AI & Soc* **36**, 59–77 (2021). https://doi.org/10.1007/s00146-020-00992-2 accessed on 01 May 25.

40 https://www.theguardian.com/news/2019/nov/18/killer-drones-how-many-uav-predator-reaper accessed on 24 Apr 25.

41 Bousquet, Antoine. *The Eye of War: Military Perception from the Telescope to the Drone*. University of Minnesota Press, 2018. https://doi.org/10.5749/j.ctv6h p332.

42 https://www.theguardian.com/world/2024/apr/03/israel-gaza-ai-database-hamas-airstrikes accessed on 12 Apr 25.

43 https://www.theguardian.com/world/2023/dec/01/the-gospel-how-israel-uses-ai-to-select-bombing-targets accessed on 12 Apr 25.

Appendix

Survey Results: Pakistan Military Strategic Culture

(275 Respondents)

Service Bracket of Respondents

Duration of Service
272 responses

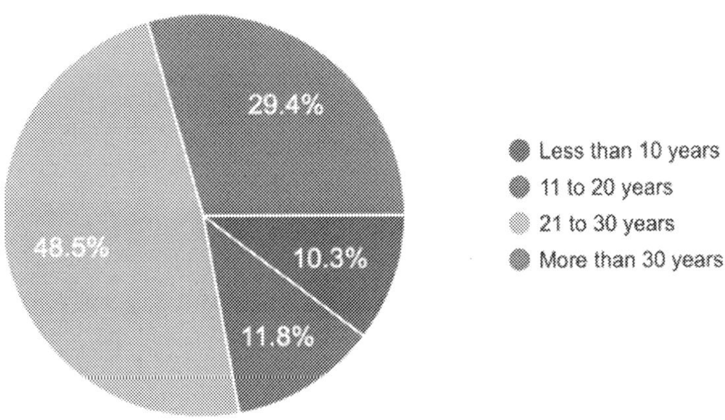

Field of Service of Respondents

Service
275 responses

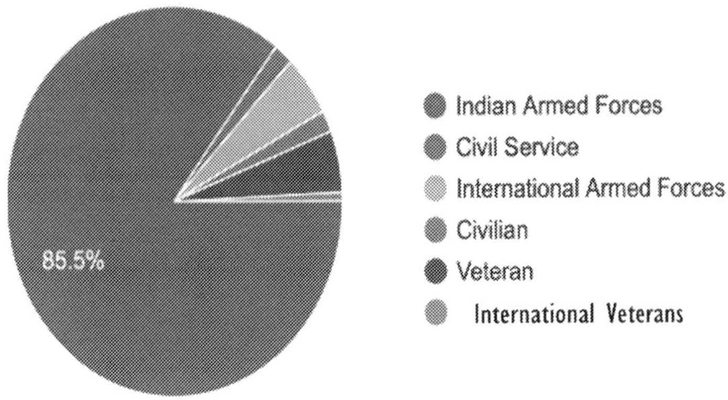

Question 1

Historical frame work for strategic culture of Pakistan Army is predicated on following pillars. Please rate them in priority (1 being highest and 3 lowest)

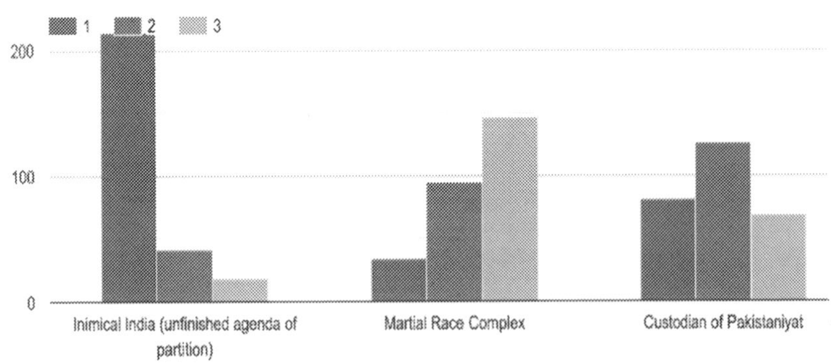

Question 2

The present frame work which influences Pakistan Army's strategic culture are the following aspects. Please provide a priority (1 being highest and 3 lowest)

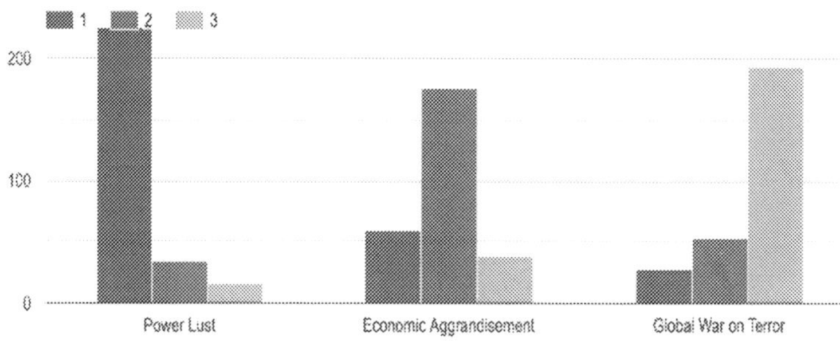

Question 3

On 09 May 23, public anger against Pakistan Army turned into a riot and Pakistan Army termed it as a Black Day. (including rioters entering the LahoL.May have tarnished Pakistan Army's image for good.

272 responses

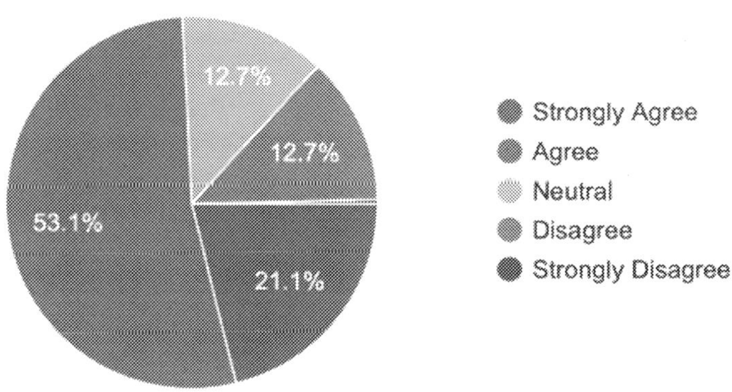

Question 4

Pakistan is predominantly Sunni, the tolerance to other sects of Islam within Armed Forces has reduced with infusion of Saiafi (wahabi) and/or Deobandi ideology in society.

275 responses

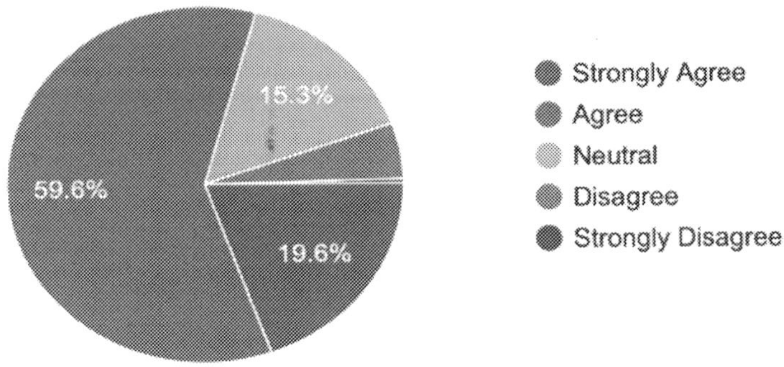

Question 5

Recent attacks in Pakistan on Barelvi and Sufi shrines and processions is indicative of an intra sect divide between Deobandis/ Saiafi Sect and Barelvi S...rian and ethnic fault lines are being exacerbated.

275 responses

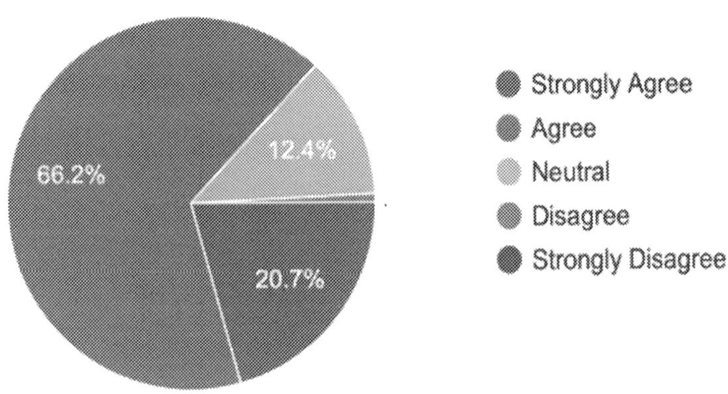

Question 6

Pakistan has ordered deportation of all illegal Afghan immigrants from 03 Oct 23. This action has creation an ethnic fissure between Pashtuns and Punjabis within Pakistan.

275 responses

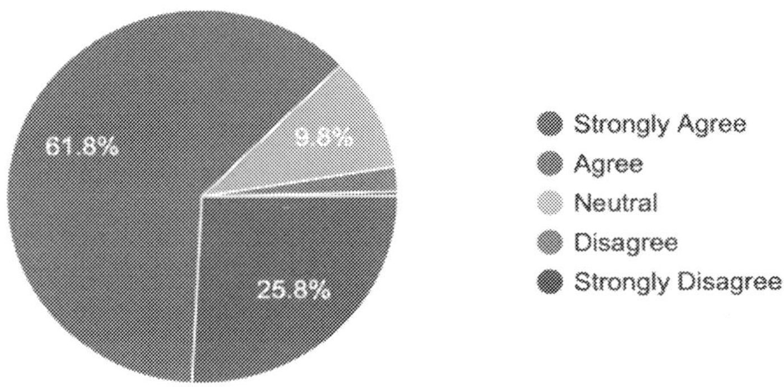

Question 7

The ethnic composition of Pakistan Army is heavily biased to Punjab with more than 50% personnel belonging to Punjab. The high handedness of Pakis.../KPK has created a Pashtun versus Punjabi divide

275 responses

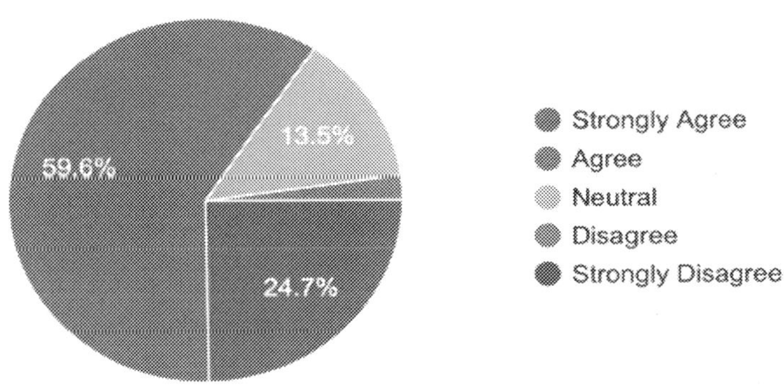

Question 8

Pakistan has used non-state actors as a tool of state policy since use of Lashkars in 1947-48 to infiltration columns of irregulars as part of Op GIBR...er terrorist operations in the initial years of GWOT.

275 responses

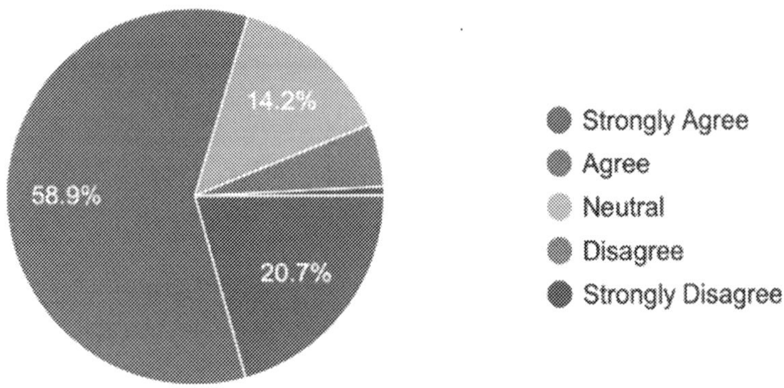

Question 9

Over a period of time Pakistan has evolved a doctrine for counter insurgency operations and has incorporated multi-domain operations as part of th...m baptism by fire and also ability to execute MDO.

275 responses

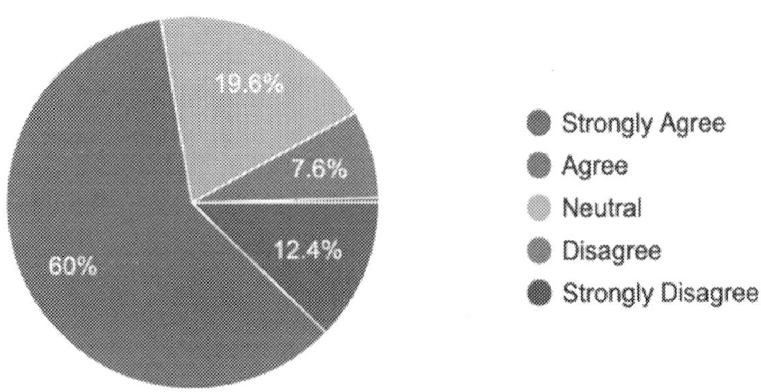

Question 10

The infusion of fundamentalist Salafi/deobandi theology in Pakistan society has had a domino effect on Pakistan Military with levels of radicalisat...SIS and AQ at lower levels including junior officers.

275 responses

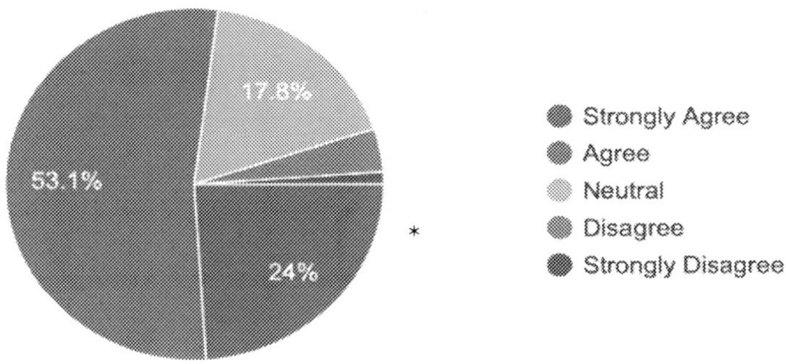

Question 11

Fatwa issued by Imam of Lal Masjid post the assault by Pak Special Forces on the mosque, denying burial to Pak soldiers martyred in combat on Weste...KPK and FATA is aiineating them from the society.

275 responses

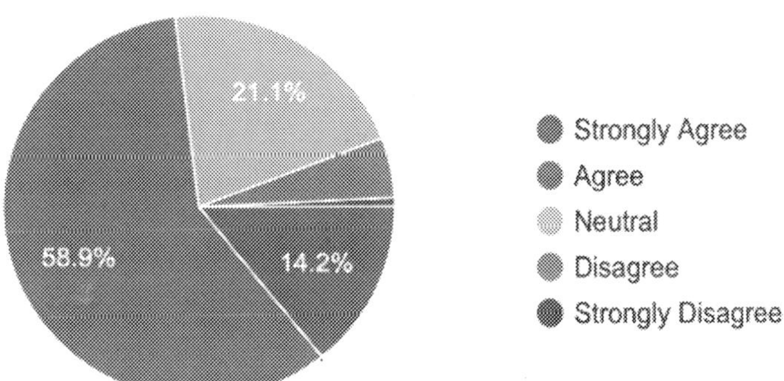

Question 12

The angst of Baluch and Sindhi ethnicity against the Punjabi hegemony creates a chasm within the Pakistan Army

0/272 correct responses

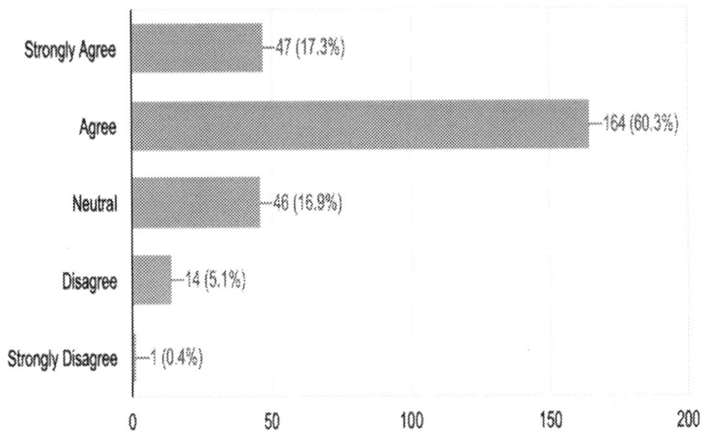

Question 13

Gen Asim Munir has a variety of challenges today, what in your view is the priority for him.

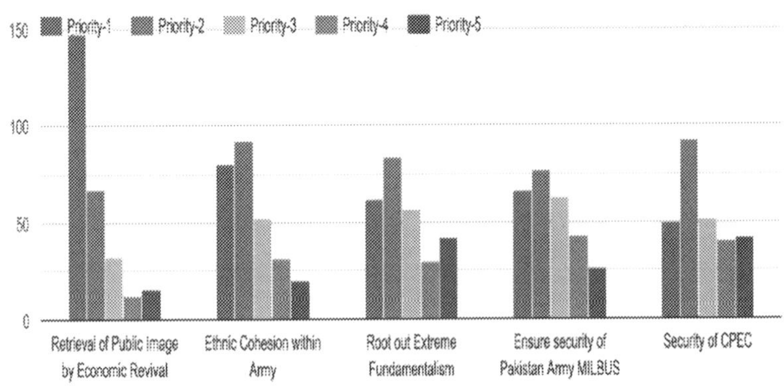

Question 14

Societal fractures in Pakistan society is bound to hamper the cohesion of Pakistan Army.

274 responses

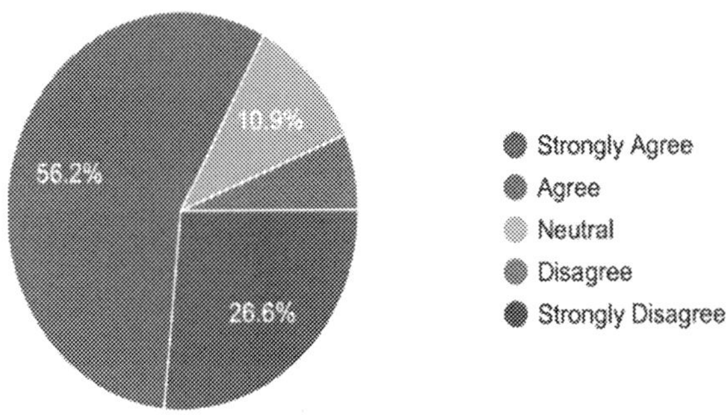

Question 15

Two strategic glues bind Pakistan together, Islam and Anti-India sentiment. Dilution of binding capacity of religion in Pakistan will affect the sta...nt Cease Fire Understanding in place since Feb 2020.

272 responses

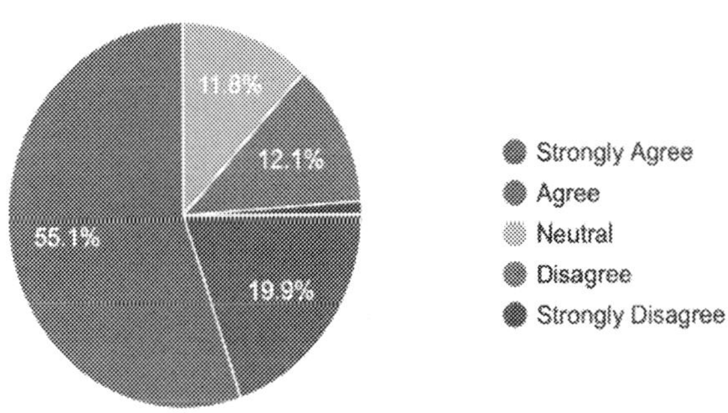

Bibliogarphy

Books

Abbas Hassan, *Pakistan's Drift into Extremism: Allah, the Army, and America's War on Terror,* New York, M. E. Sharpe, Inc., 2005.

Air Chief Marshal Muhammad Asghar Khan, *'Tareekh say kuch nahin sikha- Siyyasat aur Afwaj-e-Pakistan'* (We learnt nothing from history, politics and Pakistan Army) *An autobiography*, Karachi, Oxford University Press, 2005.

Anas Malik, *Pol Survival in Pak: Beyond Ideology*, Taylor & Francis, 2010.

Ayesha Siddiqa, *Military Inc: Inside Pakistan's Military Economy*, Pluto Press, London, 2007.

Brian Coughley, *A History of Pakistan Army, Wars and Insurrections* Carrel Books, fifth edition, 5 January 2016.

Brig. M.A.H. Ansari & Col. Mehboob Elahi, *History of Pak Army Ordnance Corps 1947-92*, Ferozesons, Rawalpindi, 1993.

Brig. Z.A. Khan, *The Way It Was: Inside the Pak Army*, Ahbab Printers, Karachi, 1998.

Carey Schofield, 'Inside the Pakistan Army: A Woman's Experience on the Frontline of the War on Terror,' *Pentagon Security International*, 2011.

Christine Fair, *Fighting to the End: The Pakistan Army's Way of War,* Oxford University Press, 2014.

Edward N. Luttwak, 'From Geopolitics to Geo-Economics: Logic of Conflict, Grammar of Commerce,' *The National Interest*, no. 20, 1990.

Feroze Hassan Khan, *The Durand Line: Tribal Politics & Pak Afghan Relations*, Stanford University Press, 2014.

George Perkovich & Toby Dalton, *Not War, Not Peace? Motivating Pakistan to Prevent Cross-Border Terrorism*, New Delhi, Oxford University Press, 2016.

Hassan Askari Rizvi, *The Military & Politics in Pakistan; 1947-1997*, Sang-e-Mell Publishers, 2006.

Henry Kissinger, *The White House Years*, Hodder & Stoughton, 1979.

Joel Hayward, *The Warrior Prophet: Muhammad and War*, Swansea, UK Claritas Books, 2022.

Ken Booth, 'The Concept of Strategic Culture Affirmed,' in *Strategic Power: USA/USSR*, (ed.) Carl G. Jacobsen, London, The Macmillan Press, Ltd., 1990.

M. Abou Zahab, 'The regional dimension of sectarian conflicts in Pakistan', in *Pakistan, Nationalism without a Nation*, (ed.) C. Jaffrelot, London, 2002.

Maj. Gen. Shahid Hamid, *Early Years of Pakistan: Including the Period from Aug 47 to 1949*, Ferozesons, Lahore, 1993.

Maria Rashid, *Dying to Serve: Militarism, Affect, and the Politics of Sacrifice in the Pakistan Army*, Lahore: Folio Books (Pakistan edition), 2021.

Mir Amir, *The True Face of Jehadis,* Lahore, Mashal Books, 2004.

Mohammad Ayub Khan, *Friends Not Masters*, Mr Books, Islamabad, reprint 2006.

Nathan Freior, *Known Unknowns: Unconventional Strategic Shocks in Defence Strategy Development*, Carlisle Strat Studies Institute, 2008.

Pervez Hoodbhoy, *Pakistan, Origins, Identity & Future,* Abingdon, New York NY, Routledge, 2023.

Ramesh Tamiri, *Pakistan Invasion on J&K (1947–48) Untold Stories of Victims*, Oberoi Book Service, Jammu, 2024.

Robin McCullough & James Fitch, *Imperial Influence of Post-Colonial Indian Army 1945-1953*, University of Vermont, 2017.

S.K. Malik, *The Quranic Concept of War*, Himalaya Books, New Delhi, 1986.

Shaista Wahab, *Brief History of Afghanistan*, Youngerman, 2007.

Shuja Nawaz, *Crossed Swords: Pakistan, Its Army and the Wars Within*, New York, Oxford University Press, 2008.

Stephen. P. Cohen, *The Idea of Pakistan*, Brookings Institution Press, 2004.

Sumit Ganguly, *The Crisis in Kashmir: Portents of War, Hopes of Peace*, Cambridge, U.K., Cambridge University Press, 1999.

Veena Kukreja, *Contemporary Pakistan; Pol Processes, Conflicts and Crises*, New Delhi, Sage Publications, 2003.

Zahid Hussain, *Frontline Pakistan: The Struggle with Militant Islam,* New York, Columbia University Press, 2007.

Zbigniew Brzezinski, *Power and Principle: Memoirs of the National Security Adviser, 1977–1981*, New York, Farrar, Straus, and Giroux, 1983.

Journals

Abbas J. Moosic, 'A Muddled Identity,' Pak Institute of Development.

Adeel Malik & Maya Tudor. 'Pakistan's Coming Crisis,' *Journal of Democracy,* 35, no. 3, 2024.

Anila Gill, 'Inhabiting a Moth-Eaten Method', *Framework: The Journal of Cinema and Media,* 63, no. 1, 2022.

Ashley J. Tellis, Christine Fair, & Jamison Jo Medby, 'Limited Conflicts Under the Nuclear Umbrella: Indian and Pakistani Lessons from the Kargil Crisis,' MG-1450-USCA, Santa Monica, Calif., RAND Corporation, 2001.

Ayesha Siddiqa, 'Pakistan Military: Ethnic Balance in the Armed Forces and Problems of Federalism,' Forum of Federations, in collaboration with the Centre for Civic Education, Pakistan.

Christine C. Fair, 'Obama's New "Af-Pak" Strategy: Can "Clear, Hold, Build, Transfer" Work?' The Centre for International Governance Innovation Paper, 2010.

Christine C. Fair, 'Pakistan's Army: Running and Ruining a Country,' *Asia Policy*, no. 19, pp. 163–67, *JSTOR,* 2015.

Christine Fair, 'Why the Pak Army is here to Stay: Prospects for Civil Governance,' paper presented by the author during Brookings Institute conference on 'The Future of Pak", May 2010.

Frank G. Hoffman, 'Examining Complex Forms of Conflict: Gray Zone and Hybrid Challenges,' *Prism*, vol. 7, no. 4, p. 31, November 2018.

'Human Rights Watch, Destroying Legality, Pakistan's Crackdown on Lawyers and Judges,' New York, HRW, *International Affairs,* 2007.

Kalin Siddiqui, 'Religious Authority and the Promotion of Sectarian Tolerance in Pakistan,' United States Institute of Peace.

Mark Briskey, 'The Foundations of Pakistan's Strategic Culture: Fears of an Irredentist India, Muslim Identity, Martial Race, and Political Realism,' *Journal of Advanced Military Studies,* 13, 2022.

P. Stan land, A. Naseemullah & A. Butt, 'Pakistan's military elite', *Journal of Strategic Studies*, 43(1), 2020.

P.C. Bratton, 'The Not So Gray Zone in South Asia,' *Comparative Strategy*, 39(1), 2020.

Pankaj Kumar Sharma, 'Conflict Over Water Between India and Pakistan: Fear and Hopes?' *The Indian Journal of Political Science,* 73, no. 1, 2012.

Parvez Hoodbhoy, 'Pakistan Army: Divided it Stands,' *Economic & Political Weekly*, vol. XLVI, no. 26/27, June 25-July 8, 2011.

Reports from Commissioners, Inspectors, and Others: [Hereafter RCIO] ten volumes, vol. 4, East India Continued. Session: June 1929-August 1930.

Safir Akhtar, 'Pakistan Since Independence; The Political Role of Ulema,' Ph.D. Dissertation, University of York, 1989.

Siegfried O. Wolf, 'Imran Khan, the Military, and the Future of Pakistan,' SADF Research Report 9, 18 July, 2023.

Smruti S. Pattanaik, 'Tehrik Labaik Pakistan and the Politics of the Religious Right,' MP-IDSA Issue Brief, 4 May 2021.

Stephen Philip Cohen, 'India, Pakistan and Kashmir,' The Brookings Institution, presented at the University of Texas, December 2001.

Sushant Sareen, 'Tehrik-E-Labbaik Pakistan: The New Face of Barelvi Activism (2023), *ORF Occasional Paper,* no. 332, September 2021, Observer Research Foundation.

Web Pages

Centre for International Security and Cooperation (CISAC), at Freeman Spogli Institute for International Studies, https://web.stanford.edu/group/mappingmilitants/cgi-bin/groups/view/147?highlight=April+19

'Commercial Entities being run by Armed Forces, https://www.dawn.com/news/127221

Guhl Jakob & Milo Comerford, 'Understanding the Salafi Online Ecosystem: A Digital Snapshot,' https://www.isdglobal.org/wp-content/uploads/2021/11/Snapshot-study.pdf

http://www.columbia.edu/itc/mealac/pritchett/ooislamlinks/txt_jinnah_assembly.html

http://www.jstor.org/stable/24905309. Accessed 30 June 2024.

https://casstt.com/an-introduction-to-converged-battle-domains-cbd-for-pakistans-defence-forces/

https://ciaotest.cc.columbia.edu/wps/cigi/0022411/f_0022411_18465.pdf

https://content.time.com/time/subscriber/article/0,33009,815599,00.html

https://crss.pk/pakistans-violence-related-fatalities-mark-a-record-6-year-high-56-surge-in-violence-recorded-in-2023-crss-annual-security-report/

https://economictimes.indiatimes.com/news/politics-and-nation/musharrafs-comment-on-failed-agra-summit-hidden-hand-says-maine-dekha-hai/articleshow/7060297.cms?fr

https://edition.cnn.com/2019/08/07/asia/kashmir-pakistan-response-intl-hnk/index.html

https://hdr.undp.org/system/files/documents/global-report-document/hdr2021-22pdf_1.pdf

https://indianexpress.com/article/explained/who-was-allama-iqbal-and-what-was-his-role-in-the-creation-of-pakistan-6080521/

https://investmentpolicy.unctad.org/investment-policy-monitor/measures/4366/pakistan-establishes-the-special-investment-facilitation-council-sifc

https://issi.org.pk/wp-content/uploads/2016/05/Tughral-Yamin-35-No.2.pdf

https://knowindia.india.gov.in/national-identity-elements/national-song.php

https://moderndiplomacy.eu/2023/10/21/from-the-two-nation-theory-to-regional-autonomy-movements-pakistans-identity-crisis/

https://openknowledge.worldbank.org/server/api/core/bitstreams/ddb936ac-9cb0-57a9-b7076928125662df/content/

https://openthemagazine.com/lounge/books/yuval-noah-harari-humanitys-storyteller/

https://pakobserver.net/bajwas-visit-helps-maintain-a-visionary-pak-us-reset-by-syed-qamar-afzal-rizvi/

https://rusi.org/explore-our-research/publications/rusi-newsbrief/bajwa-doctrine-pakistani-military-has-done-more-enough

https://sundayguardianlive.com/news/23-years-kargil-war-op-vijay-prevailed-op-koh-paima

https://sundayguardianlive.com/opinion/india-and-middle-east-seeking-an-alignment-in-bilateral-interests

https://thebalochistanpost.net

https://thediplomat.com/2024/03/where-do-taliban-pakistan-relations-stand-now/

https://thefridaytimes.com/02-Apr-2023/nadra-inquiry-reveals-conspiracy-to-prevent-asim-munir-from-becoming-army-chief

https://thefridaytimes.com/04-Sep-2023/the-munir-doctrine-blast-bulldoze-disregard-all-obstacles-to-economic-recovery

https://thegeopolitics.com/pakistans-military-extends-its-role-in-economic-decision-making-through-the-special-investment-facilitation-council/

https://theorg.com/org/fauji-foundation-group

https://timesofindia.indiatimes.com/world/pakistan/under-pressure-from-china-will-pakistan-risk-war-with-the-taliban/articleshow/111338970.cms

https://tribune.com.pk/story/1336206/upsurge-terror-army-mounts-new-nationwide-offensive

https://tribune.com.pk/story/2416010/may-9-is-historys-dark-chapter-army

https://tribune.com.pk/story/2427668/coas-centcom-chief-discuss-regional-security

https://www.aljazeera.com/news/2023/10/4/pakistans-plan-to-evict-thousands-of-afghans-unacceptable-says-taliban

https://www.aljazeera.com/news/2023/11/4/pakistan-kills-three-militants-foiling-attack-on-airbase

https://www.aljazeera.com/news/2023/8/17/talibans-ties-with-pakistan-fraying-amid-mounting-security-concerns

https://www.aljazeera.com/news/2024/1/30/at-least-10-killed-in-overnight-attack-by-baloch-rebels-in-pakistan

https://www.aninews.in/news/world/asia/pas-army-chief-asim-munir-maintains-to-not-interfere-in-politics20230309040809

https://www.belfercenter.org/publication/diplomatic-fiasco-pakistans-failure-diplomatic-front-nullifies-its-gains-battlefield

https://www.brecorder.com/news/40180175

https://www.brecorder.com/news/40252524/violent-conflict-in-kurram

https://www.brookings.edu/wp-content/uploads/2020/01/Sambandh-as-Strategy-Indias-regional-connectivity-initiative.pdf/

https://www.business-standard.com/article/international/peace-with-pakistan-will-give-india-direct-access-to-central-asia-pm-khan-121031700738_1.html/

https://www.claws.in/pashtun-tahafuz-movement-ptm-achilles-heel-of-pak-army/

https://www.criticalthreats.org/analysis/pakistans-counter-militant-offensive-operation-raddul-fasaad

https://www.csmonitor.com/World/Asia-South-Central/2024/0401/Suspending-trade-with-India-has-cost-Pakistan.-Can-the-new-government-shift-gears

https://www.dawn.com/news/1722817

https://www.dawn.com/news/266159/punjab-s-dominance-in-army-being-reduced-ispr

https://www.dawn.com/news/741890/nazariya-i-pakistan

https://www.dawn.com/news/783306/pakistans-triple-front

https://www.dawn.com/trends/raddul-fasaad.

https://www.dw.com/en/pakistan-deadly-bomb-blast-at-sufi-shrine-in-lahore/a-48646054

https://www.dw.com/en/why-pakistan-associates-terrorism-with-pashtuns-and-afghans/a-38024338

https://www.economicsandpeace.org/wp-content/uploads/2024/02/GTI-2024-web-290224.pdf

https://www.farmlandgrab.org/post/31760-pakistan-seeks-6bn-for-corporate-farming-from-saudi-arabia-other-gulf-nations-by-2028

https://www.files.ethz.ch/isn/126743/020111_Nawaz_PakistanCounterinsurgency.pdf

https://www.himalmag.com/politics/pasteen-tahafuz-protection-movement-rally-manzoor-pashteen-pakistan-rights

https://www.hindustantimes.com/india-news/india-responds-to-nawaz-sharif-s-remarks-calls-it-a-perspective-based-on-reality-101717085193156.htmu

https://www.hrw.org/news/2023/11/28/pakistan-widespread-abuses-force-afghans-leave

https://www.icwa.in/show_content.php?lang=1&level=3 &ls_id=10077&lid=6427

https://www.icwa.in/show_content.php?lang=1& level=3&ls_id=10459&lid=6670

https://www.idsa.in/system/files/book/tehrik-e-taliban-pakistan-book.pdf

https://www.idsa.in/system/files/issuebrief/ib-tehrik-labaik-pakistan-sspattanaik-040521.pdf

https://www.livemint.com/news/world/pakistan-says-will-challenge-revoking-of-article-370-1564996777281.html

https://www.mea.gov.in/articles-in-indian media.htm?dtl/Buying+peace+borders

https://www.mei.edu/publications/pakistans-military-and-foreign-policy-under-gen-asim-munir

https://www.ndtv.com/india-news/6-barbers-kidnapped-shot-dead-by-terrorists-in-pakistans-khyber pakhtunkhwa

https://www.newsintervention.com/pashtuns-join-baloch-movement-against-pak-armys-atrocities-on-baloch-pashtuns/

https://www.nytimes.com/2023/09/29/world/asia/pakistan-bombing.html

https://www.orfonline.org/expert-speak/analysing-trends-arms-transfer-china-pakistan

https://www.orfonline.org/expert-speak/fighting-to-farming-pakistan-military-s-relentless-quest-for-relevance

https://www.orfonline.org/expert-speak/if-talks-and-terror-cant-go-together-neither-can-trade-and-terror.

https://www.orfonline.org/research/azm-e-istehkam-china-s-wish-is-pakistan-s-command

https://www.orfonline.org/research/pakistan-staring-at-scary-future

https://www.poetryfoundation.org/poems/46560/dulce-et-decorum-est

https://www.reuters.com/world/asia-pacific/pakistan-orders-all-illegal-immigrants-leave-after-suicide-bombings-2023-10-03/

https://www.rferl.org/a/pakistani-taliban-land-grab-insurgency-islamabad/32595679.html

https://www.sbp.org.pk/ecodata/index2.asp

https://www.scribd.com/doc/30269950/18th-ammendment-in-the-constitution-of-pakistan-complete-text

https://www.state.gov/reports/country-reports-on-terrorism-2022/pakistan/

https://www.stimson.org/wp-content/files/file-attachments/InvestigatingCrises.pdf

https://www.tbsnews.net/worl/ex-army-chief-says-imrans-ruling-was-threat-pakisan-583586

https://www.thehindu.com/news/national/india-engaging-the-taliban-in-various-formats-says-mea-spokesperson/article67801854.ece

https://www.thehindu.com/news/national/india-pakistan-agree-to-ceasefire-along-border/article61746932.ece

https://www.uscirf.gov/sites/default/files/2011%20Annual%20Report.pdf

https://www.usip.org/sites/default/files/SR354_Religious-Authority-and-the-Promotion-of-Sectarian-Tolerance-in-Pakistan.pdf

https://www.worldbank.org/en/news/press-release/2018/12/05/pakistan-could-boost-trade-with-south-asia-eight-fold/

Keesings Record of World Events, vol. 7, June 1961, p. 18172, https://web.stanford.edu/group/tomzgroup/pmwiki/uploads/1303-1961-06-KS-AJG.pdf

Marashi Ibrahim, Re-conceptualizing Sectarianism in the Middle East and Asia, https://www.mei.edu/publications/reconceptualizing-sectarianism-middle-east-and-asia

Refugee Review Tribunal, Australia, https://www.refworld.org/pdfid/4b6fe2e30.pdf

Sharan Sunil, 'Pakistan: A Shia leads a Sunni Army,' https://timesofindia.indiatimes.com/blogs/strategic-insights/pakistan-a-shia-leads-a-sunni-army/

Sinha Rajiv, 'Pakistan Army: The Unyielding Guardian,' https://www.orfonline.org/expert-speak/pakistan-army-the-unyielding-guardian

Soharwardy Syed B., 'Wahabization-Salafization of Pakistan and Muslim Ummah, Fighting the Terrorists but Supporting Their Ideology. https://www.islamicsupremecouncil.com/wahabization-salafization-of-muslims/

Terrorism and Pakistan's response (tribune.com.pk)

'The Legacy of Lal Masjid,' https://www.dawn.com/news/1344098

www.fauji.org.pk/investors_fin.php

Index